presents

The Great I AM I AM
of the
Great Tribulation (Armageddon)
and
Rapture

By
T.J. Maryann Y.G.O.L.
2021

Copyright © 2021 by T.J. Maryann Y.G.O.L.

ISBN: 978-1-952302-98-5 (sc)

All rights reserved. No part of this book may be reproduced, stored, or transmitted by any means—whether auditory, graphic, mechanical, or electronic—without written permission of both publisher and author, except in the case of brief excerpts used in critical articles and reviews. Unauthorized reproduction of any part of this work is illegal and is punishable by law.

Author YGOL Maryann, did a street healing service for 27-years to this present, time, I am not a great bible scholar Maryann says "The GREAT I AM I AM" is written on the realm of what is professed to come talked of by many and in the Holy Bible, about the Trubaltion and Rapture. I received the perception from the lord as I started to write with compulsion and a vision, of this! reaching out to others with love, knowledge, foresight in order to prepare others for this day, No one knows the year, day time hour, Just the Lord.

The lord came upon her on an airplane coming from Pittsburg Pa. She started to write this, she was about to end the book when the virus came, an she realized she had written of this years ago which was put in her first book Your Gift of life Unity of Nations 2002 then the lord spoke of an evil force and of a virus then, with astonishment she kept writing.

As these days were unfolding in view she wrote about a manmade virus, then riots sweep over the land man made riots as she continued on with the book, with hopes that others would wake up with understanding there is an evil force Satan evil. That wants one thing our souls, as you read into the book there are ways of ending blocks along with temptations and generation curses addictions healing and more Maryann submitted this to the Publisher in October of 2020.

Maryann is not writing to judge anyone as the lord as you will read will do this.! She is reaching out to help others to get on the side of the lord as it was administered to her now in this book of The Great,

I Am I AM. A shock to her that this evil force was coming on stronger and manmade virus trying to take over all human life. Riots hate, across the Nations an EVIL FORCE.

She herself went thru much evil that used other in life on her journey to harm her and try to destroy her as she was gifted as a child and wanting to serve the lord yet The lord has the right time as she experienced more inflections like Job lost all she lost all with month to live heal issue and homeless never to think see her family again, thee children she was raising alone, the lord is good and he again brought her out of this Delema, as soon as she knew, that all can leave you, reject you, abandoned you, all but Jesus!

She then turned to him again in life, as he taught and ministered of his great love for all we all are made by him, she then enters into his call for her to do a healing street ministry for him she reported to priest, minster, rabbi and rev. all knew her and her work as she was then anointed to do by the lord doing radio shows and speaking many functions. putting her call for Unity of love Peace no destructive weapons across the Nations noted for her work Library of Congress, Who's Who.

You will read a bit more of this as she enters into the book, this is not an autobiography is a message from the lord for all of us to understand, wake up and realize that there is an evil force in the world ready to take our souls to hell with it. Will you pick.

HEAVEN -or

HELL!

Maryann speaks of the healing of the Lands as well as you will read of into the book. Her healing ministry was and is based on love and the gifts he had given her to use to help another on their way done out of love. We are all to love one another!

DEDICATION

TO

ALL GOD'S PEOPLE

As we pass together in this land,
  We must walk together hand & hand.
No matter which race or creed
  The love of God is all we need.

He is in the heart of every man
  Who wants to know where it all began.
To live, to love
  It came from the Lord above.

Passing

by Maryann

Introduction

The Great I Am I Am, is written for all who can visualize and make a picture of the magnificence of God and the horrors of evil. As you read into this, make sure you feel the intensity and the importance of every human being made by one maker. The Great I Am I Am is within the Realm of what many have spoken about in The Great Tribulation (Armageddon) - Rapture.

The wonders of our Universe are so magnificent that a painting may capture a bit of its beauty but never what the human eyes can see. It takes in and absorbs the dignity of mankind. God of all the Universe, with a wave of His hand, he made it all. A simple wave of His hand can end it for all mankind Many, oblivious to their lives, do not understand why they are here.

There is so much evil around us in the land, with such horror and darkness that many may have not seen or experienced. Yet so many are blinded, some say it will never end, some say there is not a God.

Many recognize we are in a dilemma. Recently, our world has been plagued with a very man-made contagious illness, the coronavirus, which has affected millions of people with infirmity, along with the deaths of so many.

It seems like an endless epidemic. Along with man-made rages, riots, killings all against our maker God. We hope this will unify all nations, to be at peace. and with a total cure for the man-made virus along with riots,a negative force of evil, in the Nations.There is a evil spirit trying to gain and take life souls to hell. —Are you among them.? ("United we Stand and Divided we fall we are all in God's creation." (quote from Y,G,O,L Unity of Nations)

In America, there are riots, protests for "black lives matter." It is easy to see that evil did get into the police force along with many other organizations, schools, churches, youth ministries, also many other forces, and foundations. Corruption by Satan has worked its way into many places. including hate signs hatred talking Attacking others to succumb into doing evil now, destroying buildings, tearing down statues of many heroes of our nation, who in history formed America to be a Great Nation. Fires are burning, businesses crumbling to the ground, harm, and killings of many innocent people while those doing this seem to not care of what they are doing. when our service men gave their life for our country,and all we stood for, they are out there doing this, America built on Christianity and value and freedom but not freedom to destroy,

It seems so many are filled with rages. allowing this evil to take over one-self. Is this you? Our hearts reach out to adults and young children and babies killed in these rages, and the virus as well. our thoughts and love go forward to all others who lost loved ones in this evilness of others evil that is present and has killed many. This must stop!

There are others out there with pure emotional trouble, and others who are sick mentally. And many say "black lives matter" but are out to harm police with the same wicked veracity. Others are destroying businesses and burning buildings. Fires and bombs all over, harmful beatings, and killings. Are you among them? Black life matter as the lord made us all and loves us all we are to obey the laws of God, Many of us have other races in our family integrated marriage many in life have had black and white and other races as friend, as mates to love one another creeds and gender as well. some have adopted children or mix race or others. There is love yet the evil devil is against love and has got into others to do this man made evil to one another Realize this. we are to love one another and save life not take life and destroy.

No one can do evil unless they themself do so. allowing a evil spirit to take over them This is not the way to cure, block evil by doing evil

This is not gaining anything, but loosing your souls to hell, Yes there are people who are suffering over this taking away livelihoods and costing millions of dollars, with no respect to one another. Where is love for others. People need money to pay bills, for mortgages or rent. Accompanying the riots, there is so much more sickness (coronavirus), as they go from city to city, from one area to another, spreading the virus as they are moving around. People declare this is a way to protesting, but this is not simply protesting. This we should consider this as protesting with crime and evil.

Satan is having a great time with destruction to life and and taking souls More so, with no mask no distance spreading the virus rapid with riots in America and other Nations It seems we have more sickness and death than other nations. The rest of the world appears to be containing the corona virus by quick implementations of regulations that their communities follow. Yet riots are up roaring there as well again to take souls to hell and to spread a dangerous virus to another. Do not let this be you! as we are needed to save life and soul not take it.

Many are astonished of what is happening in our world with mask a virus that keep multiplying and still riots happening We need Peace and Unity of other to be out there singing and praying praising the lord only the ones who have had shots already,not to allow evil to come to them, Do not follow Satan and his evil to overtake you,some truly loving evil of Satan with their souls going to the fire of hell doing riots, killing, not care who will be effective by the virus not to wear a mask or stay a distance and yet many are obeying the laws to keep self and others not to get sick or die. Yet there is Satan again Realize this is going on as he traps us with no freedom no way,to embrace other with love, fear to get another sick or die.with the virus a fear God who loves all and has mercy, yet man has and is destroying the laws of God. Easily we can identify these laws in the Ten Commandments. "Vengeance is mine," says the Lord! Not man's. And healing will come to all when we humble ourselves and change from our evil ways the lord shows mercy and will heal the lands.

This is a man made virus and man man riots of evil. not of God. who love us forgive us all and yet man turns to evil just as Satan will have them do. only to laugh as he takes souls to hell the lake of fire. non can make you do evil or tell you to do evil or suggest it evil is from the person themself and will not stop unless we realize the effect of this evil taking them to hell harm to another and killings as well not of God. Many are getting inpatient, as it seem so long, with some getting shots and other not, as the virus takes on many forms, mutating itself. We wonder when it will stop.It is blocking us, in so many ways to visit one another, to kiss with a holy kiss to each other to hug or have social together, fear to many to spread the virus to one another as some are carriers of it as well we all victims of a virus.

This has drawn on the nervous system of many and with fear in others as well, We must understand that we all are being affected by this virus and riots all man- made. and we need one each-other to show respect care love to each other we are all needed to help one another. not get wild up to harm instead, creating this to make it worse. It in some situation this caused a divorce,in others who went to bars,had drinks to calm them down, not sit home and drink to a excess, to get drunk or violet with too much to drink.

We all need to united in pray, as the lord will listen to pray, as we pray for self to be saved we must pray for others to realize this is not of the lord it is pure evil and pray for them to know this and be saved as well.

Many are rebelling. Or more like yielding to Satan's temptations. Satan is unquestionably in the midst of these undertakings. Obviously, not of God! It is Satan who got a hold of so many to do evil and people seem to be crowding into this lot. As they loot: food, goods, and money; and tearing down lives, burning businesses, and harming the innocent. So many people died in this, all for what? Many need help, Many need prayer, church, of all phase, and many need our Lord, and many have forgotten the ten laws of God. There are also counselors out there doing a great work for others to stay at peace with one another as the virus has created so much panic in many and fear, others reach out to churches, yet they did ban many churches for a time yet some re-open with mask and distance. we all need God's help Do we all realize this? There are myriad ways of *peaceful protesting*. Yet none seem to do this.letting the evil of Satan ruin mankind. Make Satan stop using your life! What are you doing with the life and soul the lord gave to you Who are you following God or self or another or pure Satan and what addiction do you have ? Is there a rage to want to strike back instead of Putting your hands up; and asking the lord praying to him.Yes Pray all your pray needed to change the days we are in. Pray. and follow the right not wrong.of a wonderful lord who loves us all! (John 15;17 Jesus said, if ye, abide in me and my words in you. ye shall ask what ye will,and it shall be done unto you KJV) we all have a will of God for a wonderful life. putting him first and his ways. of his truth and lite. he wants us to have life abundantly we can have this.

Yet many get wound up in a merry go round of self pity,of harm done to them by evil devil.not God, yet blame God for this. God's son Jesus, had to face evil done to him as well. As Jesus had a purpose, we all have a purpose. We are alive to do the purpose that the lord has for us his holy will for our life. our heart desires our dreams. ask the lord show you the will he have for my life and he will do so. the lord says the smallest is the greatest and the greatest is the smallest.

The lord did not want or to have others to do drugs or to sell them to another to hurt wreck the life of another, pushers, out for money. care less of your soul or their own. Drugs a cover up to face life. a giver upper of life a excuse to go forth to be and do what the lord had and has you to do. as we are all gifted in the way the lord has for us to do. In fact he said in Romans 5:8 says, "but God shows his love for us. in that while we were still sinners Christ died for us). for our salvation. All man sins. none of us is without sin, Can you toss a rock at anyone?

Bible(Peter 4;10, "God has given each of you a gift from his great variety of spiritual gifts. Use them well to serve one another when you use your abilities to help each other, God is glorified.) also(Proverbs 18:16) 1 Corinthians 13 EXB-Love is the Greatest Gift) with all the gifts we have from him and each of us do. Love means the most as without love the gifts gain nothing. read about God love for us and others from us. Love is patient, and kind love is not jealous (envious) etc. many spiritual gifts pass away,thee, go on forever (endure, remain,) are faith, hope and love the greatest is love.

During the Great Tribulation as written in this bible The Great I AM I AM as you read on into, it will speak of others, that will turn to Jesus, of all faith, creed gender realization that he is Lord, who will take us,with him in the Rapture, we need to repent and stay in the path laws of God with Jesus as we do not know, what the hour is the day or the year he may come. Be aware always of this, we have time right now to change.

Love one-another as it will break a evil force. Stan who hates love and honor to God that go to the lord, Satan hates it,and will do all to block stop fool you lie to you make you sin. We may be headed for a very hard time. Yet only God will know the time reason and season. we have time to change from our own evil we do repent of this get heal, and change from your evil ways. to forgive and to be forgiven if all change and humble themselves, and change their evil ways, then Jesus will heal the land.

We as American people can find a better way by stopping this through a spokesperson, and demand for them to look into this since so many in the police force do seem to be out of order. Yet many are in line, and put their own life out to help another a vocation they took for protection of another to follow the law as well as love for another and our Nation.There are very good police, we need a police force Yet To stop this, evil we can oblige to remove police officers from the force who are not capable anymore or competent at all.due to this evil force, or stress, perhaps drugs or discrimination and a force of anger that spread into them.

We are suffering because of the corruption of Satan, not God. Satan is the greatest liar, and he is using anyone he can get to, destroy what God made. Remember Adam and Eve and their disobedience to the lord how they had to suffer from evil of Satan as the lord took Lucifer and cast him out of heaven and with him falling angel came this is Stan who name is Lucifer and demons who have over time attack many of Gods people. they are out to takes souls and hate love for God. Let it sink in; a evil man-made virus causing others to lose their vital life organs, sickness of millions, and many deaths and still...

We are created to go forth with the love of God in us the love for others, to take care of our health and to follow our dreams our heart desires. and to live a honest moral life doing good. with all comes prosperity in all of it money and wealth.

We were not created to destroy, kill, harm life, but to save life God made and loves us.

I cannot stress enough of those who think that they are just objecting to what happened. This is so much more than just "Peaceful Protesting." This is Crime and Evil Though. Many have said, this is a warning from the Lord. We need to clearly see and know that man-made evil has been set on fire by Satan. This is why it has gotten into so many peoples in our nation and the world. others out to riots even over words someone says No one can make another person do evil only Satan evil that comes into a person who allows this to happen. Do not blame anyone but self for evil you are doing or have done. Keep a stronghold in yourself not to do evil we all know the difference between good and evil. to repent to Jesus, to be clear our souls to go to a beautiful heaven.

This is a signal, for all of us to be alert. Wake up and truly see what is going on in this present time? Does it not seem that the days of the *Tribulation* or *Rapture* has set forth? The days of evil are present in the world right now. We must stop! We must stop the evil riots and all what most citizens are doing to one another or we will be going into more. Evil: through evil deeds...signs of the end of times, flashes of the Tribulation (Armageddon, or the Rapture)

~ "The Lord says, who are called by my name, will humble themselves, and pray and seek my face, and turn from their wicked ways, then I will hear from the heavens, and I will forgive their sins, and will heal their land" ~

Some say it's nothing, although many of us are petrified! Others say, "I want to do what I want to do.! It's my life. I can do as I want with it." Not caring to wear a mask now that we need one, and keep distances we are all in this together and must help, love, and care about one another. Some are having virus party s,with music, dancing, no mask or distance. carrying on with no care at all. Yet the same people husband. wife, and others died of the virus, is this worth your life many saying I only live once I am going to have fun when others fear to even go out at all.

We have time to change the evil to good. And if we do all join in this together, the Lord will heal the lands.

Lest we find ourselves in a raging evil (Armageddon, Tribulation). Let us refrain from suffering in the dark and forever blaze of hell. For this to happen we must join in hand in hand in this world. Love one another and get along with each other, read more about this at the back of the book.

Many not caring what they do, getting high adrenaline rushes, going for evil, and thinking it's fun. Unbeknownst yet to them, they are putting their souls to hell. Pure evil from Satan slowly but surely is getting into others. It is almost as if it is moving faster as it goes along. It must Stop!

We are all in this dilemma, joining together is the first and a step away from monstrous Satan. We all have a choice...the Lord, or evil Satan. let us United with peace and love together as the time, the days,the hours may be shorter then we may realize. Yet, only God will know this. yet he says we can tell by the sign of the time. Remember we are loved, needed and wanted by our lord to be with him to let no soul parish.

Let us be still as during this time you will understand as the spirit of the Lord comes upon you, it will feel like an angel that just passed you by and touches you and you will feel his presence of flowing peacefulness as he passes by. He goes back to the world and it's like the Lord saying, "Do you follow me or the evil of the world?" and we all have a choice.

Life is precious and is a God-given gift. As we read into the book we will begin to experience a shock to what is and my come like a flash in the night of such evil not to others thinking we are not in the mist of this. yet there is a wondering insight of what is about to come one day.

In these days, and possible years to follow will be a Tribulation and Rapture, spoken of in the bible and others have written about. The Tribulation and Rapture and evil before it will appear in full bloom a start of time that only the strong will survive it. The lord will come upon each of us a touch from him of heaven, as a angle touched you, he wants to tell you, me or the world of its evil in it we have the choice, make yours the lord and stay strong and on the side of him rebuke evil.

Wear a mask and sometimes even gloves, not to spread it to others. Social distance. Consideration is a part of love and respect. We must love one another. Obey the laws of God and the laws of the land. We are unified together with all the nations on earth to protect yourself against the contagious corona virus. An evil that will one day run rapid in all nations, in all the peoples. There can be famine, no food, and water. Man is destroying man because man permits this destruction by the evil they are doing and others minds creating. Love is a strong force,that will brake a evil force. as well as living a righteous life a path of our lord, being stronger then the evil attacking at one daily,

T.J. Maryann Y.G.O.L.

Our breadth of life, one moment we are alive, and the next we may not be, in one instant, with our next breath we may be going to beautiful heaven or the lake of fire the pit of fire with the devil!

Let us start the journey of the Tribulation (Armageddon)

~with the devil or God, your choice!

A great darkness fell upon the earth; all were scrambling about with no light. It was hard to see what everyone else was doing. The darkness was eerie, it was hard to see a thing; abruptly I felt a jerk of my body and a shiver went down my spine. In the darkness sudden yelling and screaming in all corners of the earth. You can hear it felt like millions of lions roaring, ready for the kill.

Hearing high screams, crying, yelling, and gnashing of teeth, I began to shake as my body felt such a tremor through it all.

I was still shaking, standing there, looking up into the sky when there was a bright red glow with an image. Glowing in and out, as it was appearing in the sky, looking up I saw Satan himself. Lucifer, glowing in and out, flames were surrounding him, I was taken aback by this, my eyes began to water tears of fright I could feel them widening with shock. Astonished by what I have just seen...

I have never felt so scared in my life. The shock of what I was seeing and in all that was happening, the core of my body shook in astonishment and terror. I was so frightened that panic and dread was filling every fragment of my entire being. so astonished by this unbelievable horror happening, seeing this at this very moment.

There were flames all around Satan, as he was still going in and out of this. He could be seen all over the world, with snickering sounds coming out of his demonic mouth. There was smoke, dark gray in color. People were screaming in the dimness of the earth while others were chuckling with their adrenaline rising high. Those who allowed Satan to control them had such vicious smiles, and evil laughter. Taken up by such evil force in them of Satan that he was consuming their very existences.

They were falling into the lake of fire the pit of hell, trying to hold unto anything to keep them from going down into the chasm. Holding on to other bodies, and falling still, their hands burning from the blazing fire from the lake of fire You see blood running down their faces, down to their clothes. Heads were rolling, chopped off from their body. Still others were frantic, screaming, "Let me in! Let Me In!" There was not a sound to be heard from the other side of the door. The entrance has shut, the door to the Rapture with Jesus.

He gave us all a choice to choose Him or take the side of the evil of Satan in the world.

Be aware of Satan, pulling you away from the Lord. He desires for you to be in a world of evil, luring you like a magnet, pulling you into the evil. It will exhaust your soul, your inner being. To do evil is not good, and you may not realize this until you fall into the evil of Satan, and into a pit of hell.

The chortling laughter of the devil swamps the earth in all directions. By his evil that is being placed on all man to do evil as he is taking souls like popcorn into hell to the lake of fire to burn for all eternity He is well on his way to his purpose: to take souls to hell! A viciousness of evil against good.

There are no benefits in going to hell, our bodies and souls will burn there forever! Satan loves sin and is amused about it all. With no concern at all, —he enjoys and loves keeping all the fallen!— There were cars flying off the street the force of this evil where causing them to spin,as it pulled them off the roads some spinning around like a tornado taking them with it as others were falling to the ground a living nightmare, of the force of this evil.

The Great I AM I AM

We do have a choice, and yet, many do not want to believe that one day this is going to happen. It was written to prepare oneself now and to wait for the day that the Lord will come to take others with him into the Rapture. Else, we may go to Hell! Some people total disappeared as. The lord seem took one and left the other, yet all children went with him so they would not be in the Tribulation. as well as the saints others.

The grounds beneath started to open up, wider and wider. And the flames of fire were flaring so high, shooting up to the sky. I placed my hand, to my heart, this is it, The Great Tribulation. There were combustion all around Satan, as he was still going in and out with glimmerings of red, flames glowing all around him and out of his demonic mouth which was heard all over the world. laughing and as he was saying Welcome to my kingdom of Hell!!

I repeat, His image could be seen around the world with blazing red fire around him, laughing souls falling with him he was so pleased that his laughter echoed across the earth,.loving to be taking others to his lake of fire Hell! Others made the choice of Satan over Jesus, a world without the lord in it. to bring them to hell,not the Rapture,Do not let this be you.

I heard his loud voice again saying, "Welcome to my Kingdom..the. Kingdom of Hell." There were piles of bodies every few feet. Bodies were covering the ground all over the world, as the ground under began to open, more, it seemed endless were falling faster and faster and screaming! You can hear the weeping and the gnashing of teeth as they were falling into the pit of hell, into burning flames surrounding them. Will this be you? Yes, or No? Satan with all the evildoers in the world with him, falling,screaming as they fell into the lake of fire hell. Picture this...will this be you? Falling in the lake of fire the pits of hell with the devil himself?

We must take heed to this, as all will happen so suddenly. There will be others of all different races, faith or creed turning to Jesus during this time. They will learn and know that He is the only one: "He is the Truth, the Light, the Lord who will save them and bring them to the Rapture.

There will be others of difference faith Islam and Jewish etc as there will be Jewish ministering to others about the lord lord Jesus Children will go to the Rapture and not suffer the Tribulation.

And through the voice of the Lord, with a gentle touch His holy Spirit will fall among us all like a touch of an angel from heaven. The Spirit of the Lord at which time He will give us this touch of heaven. then back to the world with all evil this is to allow you to have a choice him or the evil of the world giving us time to turn to him or be in scorching heat and burning evil? Again, what will your choice be?

Satan can take over souls completely and forever. Like of Sodom and Gomorrah, disreputable having unlawful sex among one another doing all against the lord. capitals as told in the Old Testament. God was saying, give me a handful of Christians! as he destroyed The Great Tribulation of evil against good is to come. '""

There are those who rave in the evil of Satan and certainly he will take them to hell. We need to realize how much the Lord loves us all and wants to be with Him. The Armageddon, (according to the Book of Revelation in the New Testament), is the great battle in full bloom, good against evil...as the ground keeps on opening, swallowing deplorable souls to the fires of hell.

I hear the screaming and the laughter of the devil when he was burning with them. A pit of hell. Not to be able to join the Lord who paved the way to the destination we all should go to. They have not sought God. Many do not believe in Jesus or the Tribulation, the Rapture yet a day will come when they will be in the midst of it all.

Can you stop a hurricane or a tornado? God can! Or make a rainbow disappear?

In hell, you will not see the sunrise ever again! None can change this. There is no benefit to go to hell yet others are allowing themself to be devolved in evil by Satan only to loose their body and most of all soul to Satan laughing as he doing this never to be with Jesus or see your family again and others this will be permanent no turning back,

Watch what you are doing each day of your life being aware of Satan lies and tricks to consume you. as there are evil does and others doing drugs, drunks caring less about their souls and yet when this time comes they are yelling for the lord to open the door that been shuts for he said begone from the gates of heaven for I know you not.

Journey to the Rapture with Jesus to Beautiful Heaven

A great light emanated over. What is this? It was such a striking radiance and I realized we were floating in a state of existence. I knew this was from God. The sky was brighter, it was surreal. Suddenly, a white streak outlined the sky, as it fell, it filtered down to divide. Parting one side from the other. I wiped my eyes as could feel dew falling against them. I opened them wider than before and saw images of people. Some were falling to the ground while others seemed to be flying upward.

And just as unexpectedly, there was a great gust of wind and I began to spin around like in a funnel. My body twisted, my hair was blowing everywhere and the wind was warm against my face. It kept blowing in and out for a moment. I put my head down and as I was looking down I saw more bodies. Stacked up for miles. My mind kept racing: "Dear Lord, what is this all about?" Still looking down, I saw a huge sign placed on the stack of bodies. It read "SIN" with others falling so fast to the ground that has now opened wider with fire, swallowing one after another into this pit. The pour souls were screaming with pain. I put my hand across my eyes not to see this as it was going on for hours and days, it seems like years.

Nobody but evil is going to hell. And on the way to the rift you hear malicious laughter all the time; and the sight was wild with fire. Looking down there again, there were streets where evil parities of drugs and raping, shooting, and killing each other and having sex right on the streets. Women with no clothes, dancing and laughing, drinking, and with no thought of what was going on with gays and whore mongers. Adultery with witchcraft, evil voodoo dolls jumping in the fire, flying in the air, flames all around. All kinds of evil in the world of Satan. One could never imagine this happening. Children were not there. They were taken up with the Rapture with the Lord. Put inside the division of all that would be with the Lord without going into the Tribulation. Cars flying off the street; like tempests were blowing around them lifting them up and then letting go to smash against the ground with such a force. A living nightmare existed as it devoured bodies and souls. The constant mirth from Satan filling the air. This will be all over the world, not just in one nation of people but all nations of people. We must be strong against the evil force to get to the Rapture and turn to our Lord.

Flashback to:

There was a crack of lightning across the skies, with a great light which came over all. What is this? I was floating in a state of existence and I knew this was from God. The sky was brighter than usual as I observed a white streak, outlining across the sky, as it fell and made a division, parting one side from the other. I wiped my eyes and I could feel the light dew against them. All at once, there was a very loud deep voice saying, "I Am the Great I Am I AM".

A chill rushed down through me from my head to my toes. I looked at myself and the others around and I saw more people were being taken up to the sky. It has started...the sky opened and what I saw was such beauty my eyes had never seen before. He looked amazing, with such radiant colors in the sky and gold hues right under the clouds. This, I saw was for miles and miles. I kept going upward to the gate of heaven. Stunning, me with so many others, so content and joyful that we made the right choice.

There was a great light with warm winds around us, swirling us upward. It felt so relaxing as it was swirling us up to the top of what seemed to be an endless sky with the fluffiest of clouds. And behold, an angel, Gabriel blowing a horn and I saw a glimpse of Jesus our Lord, Master, Savior, Jehovah. As fast the climb upward was it was a gentle ride. We, then, carefully set down as if by tender hands on a floor made of gold. Again to my human eyes, I saw this for miles and miles. It was so peaceful and serene...so wonderful. We were so full of elation that we, again, so happy we turned to Jesus and stayed faithful with Him for this. I have been strong in the Lord. I did not deny him and I rebuked Satan, strong against that evil spirit. There were numerous of us there...so many, many, repented in the world. And, I was blissful to find millions more who loved the Lord and stood strong in Him and found themselves with the Lord in the Rapture.

A magnificent light surrounded us with an astounding brightness that looked like it was speckled with stardust. All at once, the light raised above us, and all we could see as we looked up was a staircase falling from the sky. The staircase was wide with steps shining translucently. We then saw a man in a beautiful white silk robe trimmed in blue coming down the stairs. It was Jesus with two angels right behind him and one of them was blowing a horn, Gabriel. In all of this, I wondered how I could recognize them without foreknowledge.

My heart just told me who they were. Jesus had a scroll in his hand, he raised his hand up to heaven and then he started to call each one to him. One by one names were called, numerous names, one after the other as we stood before him happy with so much love and tranquility. This place seemed to have no time nor space. It seemed hours, days or weeks but it felt like it took only moments for him to call everyone by name. Jesus is so kind and gentle, bringing us forward to Him, as all of us were so delighted to be there with Him.

Our Lord had love that generated out of him with a light so heavenly around Him and He waved His hand over us. We all knelt to Him and we then stood up as we were all being descended to Earth again. We started to go down a very placid and earnest spirit so graceful, settling us back on earth. Once more, peace came over us, now it is a world of love filling the Earth with so many others and joy overflowed.

There were smiles on our faces, we could jump and fly a bit but were gently placed down again. The earth's gravity seemed to have a mind of its own. It was there to keep us safe and secure. The grass was greener as I have never seen and beautiful gardens thrived with plants, vegetables and fruits. Tables were set-up with white tablecloths and roses in ornate vase. The earth was flourishing, upon it were trees with limbs that hit the ground in all the homes. Trees were aplenty, reaching as far as one's eyes could see. There was a structure similar to an A-frame abode surrounded with mountains and miles and miles of sparking ocean around it.

Jesus Reigns over all of us. People went about with big grins on their faces and kind words; it was a gentleness like no other. My breath was taken away by such a wonderful, astonishing feeling. There were, it appeared like, pearl lights floating in the air with the colors of the rainbow. Like big water droplets serving as a prism that colored the world. The mountains surrounding us was alive with greenness. The weather was warm and emitting a heavenly scent. As warm as it was, a very soothing breeze was all around us. Love was everywhere. Seeing a new earth overflowing with peace and love and more beautiful than ever before. Love emanated from everyone. There was always food in the gardens. Rows upon rows of all kinds of vegetables and fruits.

Gardens all over the world with all kinds of fruit trees. We were in a new world, a heaven with the devil cast out for a thousand years. We all gathered together with praise and singing glorifying our Lord as he walked among us, touching our heads and all kneeling before Him. He would wave His hand and we could all feel His wonderful Holy Spirit on and in us. We lacked nothing, as all were provided for. All loved each other. We got along with one another. The touch of heaven is so beautiful as the sky opens to such radiant beauty and peaceful spirits always surrounding us. The children were happy and so good and loving to their parents. We were all kind to one another, so loving and happy. It is so very extraordinary that no one would believe how wonderful it is. With a wonderful breeze and with ponds and rivers flowing. All the waters were with fish in them. You can just look down at the water and see the fish as they were swimming by. The water was crystal clear that you could catch them with your bare hands.

The children were delighted at this and there was a heavenly drink of water from the Springs coming down from mountaintops There were stairways up to the top of the mountains, you can look for miles and miles and see nothing but beauty. All could float in the air from place to place with an open world for all of us. We were all so happy, that we followed the Lord Jesus who we all turn to, and honor Him. Staying strong to the Lord. Grateful to be in beautiful heaven with Jesus.

We can sit on clouds and ride on them. There were happy singing and joy. We were filled with the wonderment of God. A peaceful and astonishing God, the Creator of all human life and the world.

Do We Want Heaven or Do We Want Hell??

We are blessed and we stood on the Lord's side, not to ever give in to the evil in the world. We are so blessed to be here with evil gone. for 1,000 years Yet one day Satan will be unchained and will come again to deceive the nations and this then will be the end.

Tribulation

~ evil against good - it will come one day, yet we know not when

To a wonderful Rapture...

Rapture and Tribulation are written in the Bible. - Armageddon Whatever is written in the Bible, both in the old and new, encompasses each other, making a continuous connection to the plot. Read the following chapters in the Bible to understand the narrative more:

--The Old and the New Testament--

Revelations 19-22; and 22-1-14-River and Tree of Life

Matthew 24- 25-vs 29- chapter -28

1-Thessalonians 1-Chapter-5 On Christ Second Coming --

11-Thessalonians 1-3 -chapter-v 8-chapter 2

Peter 1-Chapter-3-vs-8-of Unity and love-chapter-4-5

These are just a few passages from

The Holy Bible, King James version

Will you be going into the Rapture or with evil Satan to hell?

Do you realize this is going to happen? Great I Am I Am is a book written out of love to help everyone have a better life now and prepare for "The Great Tribulation" (Armageddon) or Rapture in life. We do not know the time, the hour, the day, or the year this will come.

The message is for all faithful, all creed, all genders, all non-believers anorectic,atheistic all life to know and that the Lord made us and loves you all of us in the world. We will be affected by this day. We need to be alert as we know not the time, the hour, the day, or the year it will come about. Nevertheless, many do know of the Rapture. A Lord that loves us all and wants us to be with Him, let us love one another! We must be prepared for this to come. As it is said, watch out for the sign of the times. We seem to be in an evil force right now. We must be strong against the evil of Satan and not fall weak and fall in the devil's lies and evil in the world. We must stay strong and hold on to Jesus, repent daily, and pray as He will bring all of us to Him in the Rapture.

We need prayer in the world as this Tribulation is going to affect all nations in the world. All our brothers and sisters of all faiths, all races, all creeds, all genders. Remember, God made us all, God loves us all. God wants us all to be with Him.

Many will be going into the Rapture, which is called the second death, the first will be the priests, the saints, the dead in Christ will rises. All who did not deny Jesus will go into the Rapture. Many who professed they believe in Jesus but out doing evil are evildoers! God says to them, "I know you not!" Remember this! The Jewish people will be with the Lord when the veil is removed. Jewish people will turn to Jesus as Savior. And Jews for Jesus and many others who may different beliefs and faiths. Yes, we all one day, will be all one. Honoring Jesus the main One for all of us. Only then, will the Jewish

The Great I AM I AM

people, get their promises filled by God. Yes, God son Jesus is Savior, the Savior for all mankind and He'll come again for the Rapture (2nd death).yet this is not the end of the world. This is about the 1000 years with the devil cast out.

Yet more will come after this time. and in the end every knee will bow and every tongue will confess that Jesus is lord. as we all reign with him. Jews chosen by God, the vial will removed as the ram in the Bush is Jesus we all will be together on the promise land and they will have the promise of the lord. given.

The same Jesus they persecuted and who endured evil with the crown of thorns on His head. With a sign placed over him saying "King of the Jews" as he died on the cross for all man's sins. Tell me, is there anyone of us who does not sin? Not sin? We all sin! What happens to the Muslims and other Jews, Buddhists, the Islamic faiths, etc.? Do they get destroyed where they left giving it a chance for the next coming of our Lord? Many good people of all faiths and creeds will turn to Jesus during this time, the days are coming when no man has a choice. Man has allowed this and the door is closed by the Lord. The tree of solvent is the Ram in the bush, who is Jesus.

His purpose for all is to be saved and go to heaven. The Father said the only way you can get to Me is through My son, Jesus. Jesus says if you see Me, you see My Father and if you see My Father, you see Me. At the very end of days, every knee will bow and everyone will confess that Jesus is Lord.

Right now, we are headed for Armageddon. Evil versus good. Where so many will be falling to hell. We must be stronger than evil. Love is the key and love will break the evil force. We are to love God, stand with Him, and love one another, all others. If we bind our family tight with love, no devil can get to us. All must change, for the lands to be healed by our Lord.

We are loved and we are on a journey in life. Let us fill it with love and good events of the Lord. Teach our children the Ten Commands of God and pray together. Teach them of Jesus and why He died for all of us. Sing praises to the Lord in keeping a positive way of life. Teach our children the love of God and to love one another. Teaching them the Ten Commanded and the salvation from Jesus, pray together for children need to know to join hands and pray and to repent as all sin. Jesus a loving, forgiving God pray for others who need prayers. In our journey and the doors of many that we encounter, our last door is to the Lord. Take care of family and friends and others who come into our lives.

Help to a Stranger

The Lord says I may come as a beggar on the street if you see someone who needs a drink of water or some food, you are to give it to them or clothes. Many are out there now who lost a job, have no money, lost a place to live in, have no car. People are fundamentally good and need others to care and help them. God may say to you, where were you when I needed a glass of water or some food? Where were you when I needed someone to talk to and pray with? If you help the least of all you are helping Me.

Many have seen angels come into their lives and who did something for them. Or at the perfect place and time was there for a reason and then just disappeared.

These chapters that follow are parts that will help with the reality of life. Human beings and the Rapture. Our minds have gotten tangled up and twisted as they are with other life spirits who have gotten so far away from the reality of their true selves.

The Lord's will for them is to be with Him. The evildoers need to change now or into nothing but evil will their lives turn to. We need to help them see, they can turn their lives about. Don't believe in the lie that you cannot get out of whatever situation you are in, because you can! Jesus loves you! and you are still alive no matter how hard you have had it or had to endure. you re alive, take in your breath of air. be happy to be able to as you go forth not in a merry go round of past. forgive let go and let Jesus (We need you Lord. honor him with love and forgive all as he has forgiven you)

Remember, life is precious. We may be well and alive in one moment and gone the next. And if we don't change now...where will we be? Now or in the time of the Rapture,

> THE PITS OF HELL WITH ALL WHO TOOK
> SATAN TO BURN FOR ETERNITY
>
> OR
>
> HEAVEN WITH ALL WHO TOOK JESUS TO A BEAUTIFUL
> HEAVEN WITH OUR LORD FOR A THOUSAND
> YEARS OF PEACE. BEAUTIFUL HEAVEN!

In time, you will understand what this phrase means "being still" when He the Holy Spirit comes upon you. He will speak to each person; His Spirit will touch us. We all will feel this from our Lord, a great Peace will befall upon us. Like an angel that just presented itself with such a stillness, it feels nothing like you have ever felt before. Being touched by the Lord then it will pass and you are back to the word. The world with all the evil in it. We have a choice.

Tribulation - evil against good - it will come one day, yet we know not when.

At present we all in American need to vote! All Americans should go to vote with no uproar, no riots! If the party they wanted was not voted in, as many are praying and asking God for him to make the final decision, the final vote is His! And with this, no riots please and hate signs and fake news. We need Unity as "United We Stand; Divided We Fall". We All Are God's Creation"

We need unity to bring peace and to have prosperity and love for one another. We are all into this together. Corona-virus, wearing masks, all the riots, no jobs, sickness and death. United together to love and help one another. During this time, we have the time to draw to ourselves, the issue we have of needing a change in self to change for the better. Life facing, not running away from yourself, not settling, denying, or going to a bar for a drink. This is not how you face yourself. Settle it now, when you can. Jesus is your Friend, as well as, your Savior. Go to Him if you need to repent, He will forgive all sins and give you salvation. Forgive yourself and allow others to forgive you as well. Satan is attacking us all, even the godliest of persons. He attacks us all. His purpose is to take souls to him. Do not allow Satan to take you over.

All hell broke loose when numerous couples take vengeance or harm each other, or, gets a divorce. We should be going in the opposite direction from an evil force. One may be taken in by the evil force and the other may not. So much tension in families over the corona-virus and we allow our energies to ignite the forces of evil in the air.

These are some issues going on at present. Whenever we think Jesus is not there for us, or, if we say, "I want to do what I want to do," we are becoming weaker and falling into sin and more sin. Keeping that up is not being able to face what we are becoming. These sins, addictions will block k your life, your love, your soul to be with the lord.Get Hooked on Jesus not on drugs and he will supply all your needs faith in him who loves you as one day we face him no other!

Sorrow fell upon me as I thought, what have I done and where will I go? My life became so toxic with sin, my heart felt empty and my burdens were heavy, my sins have taken over me as I fell to the ground on my knees and began to weep. All the drugs I did, did not help me. My addiction became stronger like a devil trying to take me to hell. I get a thrill, a high in the air but never really getting the results I needed. I fall again, not being able to face the reality of life. I get high again, a non-stop addiction, holding on to me griping my soul. Taking me to hell, for with this my sense seem to be high or numb creating me to be weak so I would fall into sex. into steeling all sorts of sin. Caught like a web, one can not get out of.

As it kept nagging me, fooling me, blinding me, lying to me, all of an evil devil. I knew my time was getting shorter when I remembered Jesus and all His pain and how much He suffered from the evil and sin of others. They hurt Him, abused Him, and spat at Him, and nailed Him to a cross. And mocked Him by crowning Him with thorns. Despite it all, Jesus looked down and forgave them, for they know not what they do. I thought of Jesus at the will of His Father gave Him as a human sacrifice for our salvation. I abruptly knelt and cried out to him.

I asked Him to forgive me for all I had done. I asked forgiveness for all the sins against Him. I cried about my shame, my lies, my sorrow, my wasted life. I wept on my knees to Him, and I heard Him say you are forgiven of all you have done, you are mine. Just then I felt a spirit leave my body, I became weak and then felt my whole body filled with such an energy bursting brand new with love flowing out of my heart and happy energy flowing all through my body.

I knew right then; I had received from Him a new life, a new beginning, and the old one is gone. And rightfully, dead. I was touched by the Holy Spirit of Jesus. I studied the word, as I reached out and helped many off of drugs. With prayers and the Lord to guide me to do so... I was free, of this addiction. going forth with a new leaf in life. by our lord, at peace, full of love, and joy.

We must change and be saved. Many can realize this, it is true. Know Jesus loves us all and we all can change. Do not ignore it nor hide from it. Face it fiercely with God. We all are not perfect and we all sin so we all need to change. It is satisfying to be set free and honest to oneself and God. Honesty will set you free because lies take you to Hell. The lord says, any man who shall stand before me and says he is without sin is a liar as all man sins.

We are on a journey in our lives. Doors open and into a room, a space in time with a part of your life being there for a duration of time until another door opens another space of time. As one door opens, there are times a door will close but the last door to open should be with Jesus who loves us all.

"Now let us enter into our journey of life and come be prepared for this now!"

What is your Choice? Do you right now have a choice? Yes! it is either the Lord to the Rapture or the sweltering heat of hell with Satan.

God's side is honest and strong. Satan wants us to be weak and to sin that way, he has you to follow the evil in the world. He has your soul for sure. The Choice is yours!

Yet, all good and bad will experience the forces of this evil from Satan. A choice of evil as his evil tangles up others in this evil thrill. With adrenaline going double-time, drawing them like a magnet, pulling, grabbing on to do evil. Wearing on the souls, the very inner being to do evil. With no resistance to the evil that is consuming them with such a force. we must know this and be stronger then the evil which we can be reaching to Jesus to help you and he will do so, Reach out to Jesus who loves you. and give you salvation.

Satan is taking souls like left and right, we must all face that we all sin, and none can toss a stone. Yet many will not admit their sin, blame it on all others or make up some falsehood in their mind. Yet profess they are godly when they are not! They will never get right within themselves, and not be happy. They may take too much food and get fat or drink themselves away. Many think they are perfect and judge others when they are hiding in their sins.

Must not be me, it is them. They never want another human being to know they are a sinner. May get wrapped up in cleaning too much, or getting into animals. We cannot judge them; I'm giving them love. It is great to clean and have an animal for a pet but not to hide behind their sinfulness. as well as jealous is a strong emotion a evil sin, as a fear of loss, will come over a person raging in a jealous spirit of another. No one can be possessive of another or try to control them. we belong to the lord, and he give us freedom of choice. if you see your brother sinning you are to tell them of this as many are blind to the sins of self. we are here to love God honor him and love one another jealous is not love. love God and one another is to love share love to others not think one should only love you and no others.

We all have a spot a place in life as a mate, as a parent as a child or grands, family or strangers and we all must love in the space we are in, some try to think they are all the wife the girlfriend the lover the mother and father or a friend all family members and are so jealous of love shown to smother hoarding love like one would be hoarding food, or clothes, etc Many even jealous of Jesus, who wants us to put them first and he will be the one we face at the end of our life to death not anyone but him a God of all. creation as he is at the right hand of the father and will judge the living and the dead None other are before the lord. his love his laws our salvation.

You can change, know that the past and the old is gone. You are breathing in the whiff of the old past, it is toxic! Today and each day that follows is a new inspiration, the newness of the Lord and all He has for you. That is right, breathe. Breathe in and out to a new day, a new life. To be as the Lord has you to be, not man nor self.

Listen to the call of our Lord and be happy that you have. Satan will be chained up for a thousand years and others for all eternity of hell. God owns the world, the tree of solvent. His only son. Jesus, our Savior, His purpose for all of us is to be saved to go to heaven with Him. The ram in the bush as at the end of the times when every knee will bow and every tongue will confess that Jesus is Lord! That will be the end this is not the end of the world this is the time of the Tribulation the Ammagdone the Rapture.

The time of the Rapture is now before the end of the 2nd death. It is said that during the Tribulation, all this evil will be going on for a long time. Evil versus good; the Armageddon. The Great Tribulation!

Where so many will fall into the pits of Hell. All mankind, we must be stronger than evil. this message given to many to write of, I started this book over a year half ago and in the mist of a virus starting as it went along to more evil riots etc,

Yet many who love and stood strong against the evil bonded with their families and others with love. Doing good and keeping on this path will usher us into the Rapture. Love God and Love one another.

Can our minds possibly visualize our world with so much evil in it? A car could be pushed with this evil force. It can turn it upside down and run more cars off the road. With others running in the streets doing evil. These are the days of the Tribulation the Armageddon- evil against good!

All around the world, evil will be present. We are in a time of life where we must all wake up for our souls' else end up in hell. With evil Satan having a heyday, going on from place to place. Sickness may befall us all that has no cure. Illness after illness, disease after disease. This evil can take us down by taking away food and water, polluting our world with more germs than other areas. Other areas may dry up and become deserts. Many will die, all because of evil. Yet the Lord says "if you humble yourself and turn from your evil ways, I will heal the land."

THE Great I AM I AM is who God said he was when asked the Tribulation and Rapture is called the second death, or the Rapture. Many called the Lord by different names. Yet, pertains to one God, the Creator of us all, and one Jesus the Savior of all mankind. All souls rightfully belong to Him. We should respect all names the Lord Jesus is called. Any names, as I said Joshua Master, lJehovah, Christ, Al Mighty God etc.

Teenagers –Adults

I work with kid like this and you have no idea and what i wrote is true. i took other with me out of situation like that and got them well and into careers and service and schools on own and able. some young kids died here on this side of Fl with heroine they lace it now to make you die ok.

I as well want to put in the book about Jesus speaking of himself as a beggar on the street etc. I will find it ok. We must not be afraid to pray for a homeless person or give them a drink or a few dollars with a pray and tell them for food you can mostly tell if the person is on drugs or drink others without job and desperation, I tell them to stand back from my car and I have window rolled down now and then I ask them if they want a pray all want a pray then I pray for them to have a place to life and job and food and of course I do ask if they are on drugs or addiction they will tell you most do if you tell them I will pray for you, and pray it pray to the lord for him to take them off the drugs and to help them stay strong, give them a place to live and food and work they happy with this ad if you have a few dollars give them for a food or drink I give my tides to the poor hunger I meet up with.

Our teens especially are being drawn to reach out and rally for the Lord against these evil forces. Join in with other teens, even younger adults. Pray for things to change. As our teens and young adults join in. They will be filled with the holy spirit with love joy of having others turn to Jesus and realize their true purpose in their lives. They can also pray for the salvation of the souls. We need to bring them all to the Lord.

Teenagers are wonderful and they have great energy. It is such an inspiration to be able to do this for our Lord, our God draws them to Him...and He will. As you go forth and pray, the Lord will lead you to reach out and pray for one another...so do so! This is wonderful!!! The fear of the depleting of our environment and the end of the world is not true at all. i saw children crying and sad and believe we are going to die in our earth all over the environment. and we must not have cars to burn oil or gas. we must do something of our water yet there is water pure yet God is the sign of the time and it not about the environment or a sun to fall or a moon to not shine for we polluted the earth.

Yes we can do better not to put waste of any kind into our oceans. to clean up our cities and seem most of all San Francisco to get aid to the homeless to get and renovate empty building to put in beds shower food clothes and get them who are on drugs off of them into a special hospital for this, and others out to work in the street that they all just polluted filled, with disease of waste, even given needle for the addiction they have they can work to clean up the street, and other areas that the homeless made a huge mess in, being treated like sick cattle, even sick animals are being treated better than many states have treated homeless there. let us help my getting homeless others to know they are loved by God and worth all to him and self and others. get them a bed to sleep on and help them with the life they do have yet to live and be positive and productive in with meaning and purpose in their lives bring them in to a clean environment to live in where they have good shower food and others to talk to counseling and other to pray with a daily service to hear of a Jesus who loves them and is first in the life of all, and others to help them.

This can be done. let us solve our trouble not add to it more. Many have lost all like Job, in bible others have been rejected or out of work or had illness to leave them with no job no money no family some parted from the family not able to keep with them. many suffer abuse and cannot seem to let it go out of them. needing pray counseling and healing of this worthy of all. to go forth in life to accomplish,

The battle between good and evil is. It is a battle between two spirits. The Lord, who is always good and Satan, the evil one. God brings on good and love. Satan brings on grave corruption. He came to hurt, lie, and destroy and will fool you. He does all he can do to take your soul to hell and go against good. The only way to overcome this is with JESUS!

As you reach out with love, know we are not in the day of Peace and all this global talk of our dying environment, all this talk of no oil, no cars running on gas. All sorts of things are wrong, as the days we are in right now are days off a contagious virus, and evil riots, and don't you ever let go of the fear of our environmental and realize this is what is truly happening in the world because of this.

All talk of this is wrong, yes we must take care of our environment yet this is a Pray God we will change, in a Unity of love for God and one another to forgive and with total honest forgiving all to God and to another and Change, as to be forgiven to honesty repent of this sin there is a Change! The lord will forgive yes, more then one time yet he said to go and sin no more. He will if you do turn you over to a rebate spirit which means he will not listen to you again To be forgive or forgive means Change. we know the sin and we must call of Jesus to give us the strong hold not to do it again, strong not to allow the devil to weaken you to this as he will.

The Lord is reaching out to you. He wants you with Him. He is the God who can make a rainbow with beautiful colors or he can create a hurricane, or, rain and floods similar to the time of Noah's ark. There is a God above who creates stunning sunsets to watch. Every single day it can be different, too. And with God comes the birth of a child. A new generation, a new hope. He made us to love. He is in full control. Man upsets Him for doing wrong and with all the evil that has and is and will happen. All is his, all human kind all animals of the earth and birds in the sky all fish in the waters all the entire earth and all in it belong to the lord. yet he cast out to the earth the luthifer devil as we talk of and with him came others who are demons. Satan is for evil and truly in the world we do not live in heaven we live in the earth and in it is a evil force who has and will hurt many called Satan and know working double dime to take us all to hell,

Yes, if evil people keep destroying buildings, and lands, and waters, with chemical sprays. If a man produces a virus to kill millions, or, if people will destroy the land the holy ground we walk on and the air we breathe. Probably, chaos will endure. We need to remind ourselves that everything is from the Lord, the flowing waters, and the lands that give us food, shelter, and security. Now that man is presiding over the earth...it does look like chaos. Yet when the Lord takes over all, we will have everything and be extremely happy.he is the light of the world and in all do us we do have Jesus be free to allow his love, his light to come to you, shine in you, out of you, and around you. each day.

The Great Tribulation, Armageddon will be so bad that others will be running around doing so much evil. Many though will be crying out to the Lord. The Lord said, if we humble ourselves and change from our evil ways, he will look down and have mercy and heal the land. This is when evil so great and many faiths turn to Jesus. If we turn to Jesus, evil will stop and Rapture will come and the Lord will heal the land. He will restore all to a beautiful natural state again, yet many may not listen to the call of our Lord! while we still have time.

> Romans 12 vs 21 Do not be overcome by evil, but overcome evil with good

> Isaiah 5-20 - Others call good evil and evil good. They put darkness for light and light for

> darkness who put bitter for sweet and sweet for bitter

1 Corinthians 15-33 - Be not deceived :evil communication corrupt good manners

Worry about yourself and get right with yourself and then reach out to another and help others as well. Nothing to worry about if you have given your life to the Lord and has repented. Sincerely ask Him to forgive you. Are we sinners of course we are. We need to accept that we are sinners, all human beings in the world, so we all, in reality, need Jesus to give us salvation. He will provide us healing and bring us with Him to the Rapture.11 Corinthians 12 vs-9-My grace is sufficient for thee, for my strength is made perfect in weakness.

In the world, there are so many good people, devoted people doing amazing things, to help humanity and themselves. To gain forth and prosper, yet during this time even the saved will be tormented by the evil. It will do all it can to break you down. hold on tight to the lord, he will see you through this, Also, many who do not believe in Jesus and think He is not there for them may have called on him, and he was there but allowed evil to step in as in life there is evil from others as Jesus himself had to face this. But the fact is, Jesus Himself had to endure evil from others who hurt and abused Him so badly.

Man had nailed Him to the cross. He said that all we have to do is to forgive them for they know not what they are doing. we must forgive, at times it is very hard to forgive. yet we then think of Jesus and love and know we can forgive. Many say look they did wrong and rotten to me, yet God bless them. The lord said I will pour my blessing amoun the just and the unjust for the unjust have asked the lord to forgive them and he then will bless them. who can toss a stone at another none. as we all make mistake is life and many have suffered for the mistake they made,many have repented from it and Jesus turn and bless them Misake are made daily yet if you pray and ask the lord when you are about to do something even a marriage to another and the lord show you not to do this marriage or other and you do not listen to the lord you just made a mistake and you will many accept it and yet suffer in ways for this, once they go to the lord with it he can and will bless you even if you have made a mistake. as many mistake in life have put us in bad situation to get our spirits upset to sin and to do thing we wouldn't have done at all.

There are generation curse as well which brings on a twisted mind as evil got into them ~ Satan. God had to show us that evil is present in the world and evil will hurt or harm us, even kill us. But He will forgive.All man face tragic, evil, hurt pain loss, abuse rejections from evil. anger killings rapes all from evil not of God The lord will heal you from this and bless your life. There are sins of our parents called generation curse, how do we get rid of this ? We must pray it off so it will not effect to harm others from one generation to the other. Can this be broken ? Yes a generation curse can be broken, by pray one must pray it off. asking the lord to bake all generation curses now and for rest of all generation to come and he will do so. we need protection of other evil as well. in the later chapter of the book I have given you God's way of protection to oneself we are precious to our lord and he finds us ways to combat evil.

"We all have a Soul"

Satan wants your life and soul; he wants to get your soul to hell. Be aware of this. Love is the key that will break an evil force. Satan is against all love and is out to take souls with him and use anyone to take our soul to hell. Wake up to this, be not blind to who you may be with or what is part of your lives. Satan is against families who love. He brings disorder and chaos to husbands and wives, brothers and sisters, and even mothers-in-law to mothers. He will raise havoc, to hate each other and propagate the seeds of evil. Satan will do as much as he can to cause such discord. You need to know it right off and do not let it happen at. Rebuke him, be strong against the evil, walk away from it, pray, go in the other direction. Show, act, talk about love to one another. As we go through the journey to the Rapture and life before it happens. Stop! Listen and reflect. Trust God and bind with the bond of love. Do not let him fool or come over you to do adultery and to steal and such evil and other not to love one another.

Are you an Inlaw or an Outlaw?

All Satan does is destroy and not to have you share love, remember we all have our weakness, a flaw for the love of husband, wife, mates, children, mother, father, others you are close or have a place in our life. All have love that is special. Satan wants you not to love or share love or have love at all. He is evil and a liar, jealous, and causes division of many. He is against love. He will do all to destroy your love-soul, leaving you empty-hearted. He wants you to lose all your resolve.what you bind on earth you bind in heaven and what you loose on earth you loose in heaven so make love a strong bond. honesty bring a deep love and a channel to the lord be honest in all you say, do and think,this will bring you to know God in his fullest a Godly life,

Do not listen to anyone who will try and many will do so to fill another up with lies with hate. No one owns anyone; the only one we truly belong to is Jesus. put your strong hold inside of your mind, heart soul no one will be able to influence you to do evil at all you will reject them of this. Just call on to Jesus and tell Him you need Him, walk away in the other direction of evil.

HONESTY WILL SET YOU FREE! Even as a child, we can be dishonest. "No mom I did not do that!" "No dad! I did not do this." All the while the child did break the toy or ate all the cake. As a child you fear rejection and that fear makes a child lie. Even as teens and as adults, at times, the feeling of shame makes them hide their mistakes and faults. We all tend not to admit to it, own up to it. This embarrasses us that we would rather lie. At times, kids may "steal" or take things for their own. They feel bad…we may feel horrified by what they did but we may find out that they just need love. They need our attention and our love. If kids get jealous, they fear the loss of love. Hold their hands and pray with them. Teach them the Ten Commandments of God and Jesus. Remember, most times, if we handle them with love, the child will respond and tell you the truth. Let your child follow his or her dreams, the desires of their hearts, and help them to achieve these.

With love, determination, positive, faith they can accomplish this. be supportive of your child's dream without inflicting what we want them to be Children are blessings. Teaching them honesty and living honest lives is a blessing to them. They will feel and value this trait as it brings them to a higher level with the Lord. They will feel free and strong. loved and to love to follow the desires of their hearts with accomplishment allow them to get there dreams and if on the way they may find another vocation they would not have found if not to follow their dream to start with, and many follow this, as wall as others to follow the dreams they have and fill there heat desire, Right now our children are suffering,the empty hrs of what can I do, not fully understanding, just what is going in our world.frantic some over a virus they know not truly from where, and how it is effecting many, It is up to us the parents to have them not get stress out fears that will upset them, Just pray with them, telling then you love them and the lord will find way to stop it as he loves us all. and this is not of him, its been done by a huge mistake in a lab, with scientist who were making something and it got out.

So many say from China a country very far from us, yet it traveled to us, Do not worry, we in the country's will find a cure for this just like you had a shot for chicken pots and other we will have a shot for this as well. You will go back to school when they know it is safe for you to go back, If you are a stay at home mom you can do Home school for them, it seems like not many children are getting the virus, so perhaps school will open again, wearing mask and seating distances may do it for them. We ask that in the school system they will put up the Ten Commandments of God.

It's not our way, it is God's way, and His way is the right way.

If you are following the Lord, you are on the right path. Many do not want to admit sins. So if the sin is not confessed to the Lord, one is unable to repent. And if one buries one sin, after a time, he or she will do more and bury them as well. Not to ever admit sins can tire you down. Jesus can release you from all of this. You will may feel overwhelmed in your heart. It may have come from abuse or rejection or loss or loneliness or harm. Jesus is there for everyone. Don't ever think Jesus is not there for you.

You who needs healing. We cannot escape a life without situations that the devil will throw our way. He can use someone somehow someplace to hurt us, harm us. This is evil and God is exactly the opposite.Yet know for sure there is a Satan in our world not just God as Jesus had to experience the hurt pain evil done to him. Yet he forgave non would harm you if they where not influenced by evil and a twisted minds and hearts or a generation curse. from one generation to the next. can we broken with pray to end it in other generations. to come. or perhaps abuse done to them they repeat.

Satan wants you to have a shell covering your love in your heart, he wants you to hate and turn away from Jesus. He wants you to go and do drugs or get into a pity party. He wants for you even to die in the streets or anyplace. This is what Satan wants not the Lord who gave you your life and loves you. To be healed is to be happy, go forth and forgive the person who hurt you or rejected you, forgive them for it was not them. It was the evil Satan that got into them to draw you down for he saw you are a special, loving person. He is against love and good.

This is Satan and he is after your soul so he can entice you to go to hell. He tries to instill in you an addiction to drugs, he fills you with hatred to kill and to do all sorts of evil to yourself and others. It is not God! It is Satan and anyone who harms you, it is not them, it is the evil that got into them. Because they allow it to happen. If you have sinned against the Lord, even out of desperation. He forgave you, ask anyone you hurt to forgive you and forgive yourself. You know, no matter what it is that life has been thrown at you, God himself will take care of it.

God watches over everyone and pours out blessings in their lives. Some may have had a child who they have given up for adoption. Even if they did not want to do it, but it happened. Know that God is watching over this child. With so much going on with technology and DNA testing, one day you may, like many, be able to see that child again. You may be shocked to know that the child is having a good life. All because you asked God to forgive you and He is watching over the child.we have a understanding Lord who see all know all and can do all many have done thing in a desperation and no one to truly help them or want to do so or for other reason mistake are made sin come into it Lord know all and forgive us all. as he will bless us as well we must learn to let go and let God for he truly know best Trust in the lord who will not fail you.

He will touch you with His love and free you of all sin once you repent to Him. You will feel the Holy Spirit come over you and set you free. The Lord talks to many, telling them they are forgiven or to go out and serve Him and to start by saving souls for Jesus! Many are lost but found for they have searched their life over and not to know who and what they are searching for is Jesus in them the holy spirit of the lord when you have done all your have gone to the end of the line and realize there is a Jesus that can help you love you forgive you,

As you give your life to him on knees surrendering your will to him giving all self to him my mine my heart my soul my being all of me belongs to you Jesus and asking him to forgive you he will touch you with the holy spirit of him as you cry out to him all of myself belongs to you lord let your will be my will and my will be your will as you watch the lord guide you to the will he has for your life to follow God will in life for oneself will make you happy as you are in his will if you have one doubt ask him again and he will show you the will he has for your life and all from God is good.

ONE OF A KIND

Remember you are one of a kind. Imagine this, "one of a kind" no one else is like you. God makes you like no one else. Even identical twins may be similar in most of their physical attributes but they are different as well.and have souls that our their own as God will for their life as well Twin is a Twin but life and soul are separate. Are you a twin or someone you know is a twin.

The Lord needs us all with him, all creeds, faiths; needs Jewish, he needs the Muslims Islam and the Christian and Buddhists, atheist who say there is not a God. words, hurt feeling, think the lord abandoned them look what Jesus had to go thru himself and his father present to show that there is evil in the world other get affected by a devil used to harm another not of God and yet Jesus forgave all who abused and torment him as he hung nailed to a cross a cross he had to carry to his own death being abused by evil on the way. We all experience evil and like Jesus we have and must forgive all. as he did. he died for all man's sins, and anyone who ask him to forgive them will be forgive and set free as we must do.this. There is one Jesus one of a kind who love all of us. he wants us to know this he died for us all,his purpose in life for all human beings salvation. as all mam sins. Yet evil is running rappid it must stop!

Doors and rooms in the world will open to you, for more opportunities, for your career, As soon as the corona-virus that is in the world, is under control and others have been administered the sermon in a shot for this. protecting them from the virus. yet many do have weakness in them and some may get sick from the shot, effects may happen there seems to be no way to truly analize if they will or will not be effected with hopes none will get sick from it. we need to all join together in prayer for this to end and for evildoers to stop whatever it is that they are doing. or what to scheme to do, not of God.

Some of this hate, goes back to the start of the election of our President Trump, we know that many wanted him or his running mate Yet we as intelligent people God made. know we must concede to whom the lord had for office of President for many prayed about this as many ask the lord to place who he wanted in office God selected who he wanted, and regardless of all may not have been who the other partys wanted but God made the choice. Yet others try to say it was not legal and Russia had something to do with the election here in America which they proved did not Yet hate sign and riots started then over this. trying to impeach a President that the lord had in office for his reason not man.

This was and is today for all the riots that happening and happened is not of God as it is not peaceful protesting and to concede to a President in office. who doing it others not God or others who have conceded evil just in another not of God and none can make a person do evil just Satan and this was then starting to take place it's not the partys fault it is the person fault. to do evil for what,

Many in the world have wonderful talents, we must learn how to share, learn appreciation and interact with one another. Some talented people share their talents and they feel gratified and grateful because of the beautiful experience of sharing. Bear in mind if you have a light and you put it under a rock, it cannot shine under a rock. Remember, God is love and wants us to love each other so just reach out and love someone today. Love is not a sin and sharing is caring. There are so many beautiful people doing wonderful things with their lives. Meeting all races, in my life and praying, for and with all races and creeds, joining in many different faiths. Love is the key. If we all love one another we will realize that healing and blessing come from the Lord Jesus. We need to acknowledge this and all will be saved. From other faiths to Jesus with healing and blessing, I was a part of many to reach out and pray and help others. Black, White, Asian, Brown, Red, and Yellow.

It's not skin color, we are human and we are all brothers and sisters in the world. God made us all, the peoples from different backgrounds and nationalities. All of us and He wants us to love one another, as well as follow the 10 laws he sent for us to follow. Will hate, meanness, and, vengeance, take you to the Rapture? No, it will not! You will not go to the Rapture. And you should know, you do not want to miss it. It may come in the blink of our eyes it may come from evil. Evil will only draw more evil, to tribulation!

BLACK LIVES MATTERS

Others cannot understand what is happing in our life's they are consumed ; with the non-reality of the state the world has become reflecting on non-believers.

It's like a hilum balloon, floating aimless into the sky,taken up by the presence of a force of wind tossing them two and foe, against the toxic waste of human life,as it exists with, no realization of this force of evil against the good of God and the evil of the devil taking souls with him,

More and more evil has up roared. as we saw others pop shooting from car innocent children being shot. there is no moral value to respect life. no care, no love. no value. for our precious gift from God our life's so many trying to demolish good. many with fear of environmental change when it is change of evil to good. We are a wonderment to the lord as he makes all of us one of a kind, and with special gifts from him, bring out the wonderment of self and not allow Satan to tell you other as the lord has something special, he has for you to do. as he has for all he made. and it happens in his time.

The generation of the black race paved a way in life yes, many blacks were slaves and with the spirt of the lord and his love, as many whites loved black people and still do today, we had a black President and black actor and entertainment many did well in the black race. so, this about decimation is not truly true at all for many and not with the lord.

What about other nationality who came here by boat from other country they had nothing but self and some few clothes and many could not talk English at all. many had to learn and so many of all race and creed came here and American build on Christianly what is now is all, creed gender nationality we need to stick together in a harmony of Peace and love standing strong against this evil that has run rapid trying to take our souls to hell for us to hate and fight against one another it is not anything but Satan so let us all face this. by being strong against it and show one another love.

love will break an evil force.

Parents who are overbearing unbelievable not to allow their child to grow only controlling them blocking them from having friends going with other teens doing things to expand their life they yes, it is wonderful to bring your children up in the lord and to teach them of other who fall like drunks in the street or drugs. nourishing your child or children is one thing but to dominated and possessive even some jealous leaving your child teen to just then will rebellion and then downfalls begin to have before one know you begin to argue and feel like you lost control telling them to leave or told to go at times into a street.

A street homeless where they have nowhere to go. as desperation steps in for them to survival and doing things some teens just will do out of desperation wreck some so young and out to a street being taking advantage by sick people are looking to take advantage of a young boy or girl using some young girls for sex and pulling them to be a lesbian and other boy the same using for sex and many homosexuals bring them into be gay some girls turn to prostitution and some young men the same,

There are others who will give a teen or an older man work to make money but as soon as they do there is a joint or crack heroin something for them to take,buying from the person who just hire them to work, giving them money getting them hooked on this never-ending battle,soon work and drugs. We do not want this to happen to our child or children, let us love and pray and listen to the needs of them and take time out to be with them do special events with our children make a happy children's days sharing love.

Many have died in the street. Parents need to sit down and talk with your children as children and as teens,to respect each other talk of what they feel want to do with their life dream and if you do not like the dream say nothing as the child dream is his and you must be supportive of this heart desire to crumble a dream or to find fault with all a teen will do and put them down is not good at all.

Love not rejects what they may do or say if it is not what you want,who is first ? God who makes us all is first giving you a gift a child or children he is first the child or teen we are responsible to teach them of the lord. with a journey for their life the lord has for them. chosen to have dreams heart desire to come true for them be a asset in your own child life not a hinder spirit be positive and happy with the gift of love and life God gave with special gift he has given to each of us.

Learn to pray with one another and join in healthy groups and happy things to do. and together as well. Bind your family with love. caring for one another not judgment to each other anger strife discord spoil or try to take over their life's Pray,in the morning and during the day and at night pray as much as you want to or when you may want to but pray a family that prays together stays together...

You are wonderful, the lord made you wonderful get to the inner of self as you put joy in your soul your life forces up to uplift self if you feel rejected, know that Jesus loves you and will not reject you it's the evil of others not the lord who harms another, as Jesus had to experience evil himself and yet turn and forgave. you are special, you are one of a kind, so it's up to you and to shine in you around you and to you with the sparks of our lord. who loves you, Trust in the lord who will not fail you in life.

The lord speaks in ways to us, guiding us. If we have a decision to make even for a marriage. ask him to show you if it is the right thing to do or not, if not the lord usual will come upon you or something will happen to show you no. and if it happens to show you no then do not do it. or you make a mistake goes for all we do. to make a choice about if we go as many, without a pray to the lord, yet we know for sure it is the right choice.

Blessed are you! many do have a inner gifts from god for this. as i said before we are all given spiritual gift us them and for another if we do not know and make a wrong choice. then know you are going to have issues and mistake give you hurt pain and some marriage broke up, and some stay for the horror of a life together filled with discord. yet even a mistake God will bless you in the moment you go to him with it, he has love mercy and will change things for you, a mistake can turn around with Jesus and be a blessing instead. Never underestimate the power of the lord.

As follows are some points in my own journey of life the lord show me, his power of his love, to bring love back, restore, bless and heal.

God loves all, so to our Lord all life matters. He does not discriminate; He has made us all.

I would not be writing this book out right now if a Black family did not find me in a street, homeless. in D.C I lost weight and my health deteriorated. with kidneys having months to live I lost my family and I was raising myself alone. I lost my job, my home, my money. I was like Job I became homeless, with pain and sickness in my body, my brother and sister of a different race found me and took me in. They helped me, brought me home with them, and nourished me. They even brought me to a Miracle Temple in Washington DC, where a woman who had the healing gifts, prayed for me. I was the only white woman in an all-black church. Did they love God and me? Yes! I was healed by the Lord to keep the one-third function of my kidney. `I lived on to see my children again and still now, after so many years, I thank the Lord for He was wonderful to my children and myself. My children reached out to help others. And all did have wonderful careers and life, family of their own children and mates loving the Lord and helping many.

Even adopting children of mixed races and black race, touching the lives of so many teens and children. God made it a point to bring them back into my life as we reached out to one another, even my wonderful grandchildren. Jesus blessed us all as i was healed yes, and went on to college. In a addition page in the book I will tell you of the journey i had with our lord. I did bring my children up in our lord to know and love him first, others and self and keep healthy so they could do the purpose the lord had for their life and with this will come prosperity in money as well The Ten Commandment of God and to be honest. we all were blessed with Gods love.as love is in all men's hearts They thank me to bring them up into the lord. Jesus.

Yet sadly we can be hurt abused and bring a crust over the love, to have burdens and grudges along with sorrow. The love of the Lord is special. We need to put Him first. and to forgive as he did is a blessing to be forgiven of sin and to forgive another who has hurt you. to be set free and to go on to know you have your gift of life no matter what has happen you are still alive to follow your dreams and to do the will the lord has for your life. Jesus make a path,, a way that i would serve him and did for over 27 years faithful to his calling of him, as i did a street service healing ministry.

The lord made us all human being he loves us all we are unique in our nature, to love and know him. Yet many may seem not to realize this yet, true.

IS IT GOING TO BE GOD? OR SATAN EVIL?

It is hard for all to have to wear a mask and stay at a distance not to get this virus. It has been stressful to many and put many on edge. Who would ever believe in our time we have to wear a mask and social distance and experience riots? Burning down things? No wonder all are getting frantic. We must do all to reach out, wear a mask and glove if needed, help each other overcome with love and pray for hope and show concern to help out whatever they are facing today. Pray for one another and keep loving.

We are living in days of wonderment, some area with weather issue out of the blue different. we have time to ponder over our life, facing the inner of our souls, getting to face issue and sins not avoiding them making changes in your life and repenting of sins. Picking up the word of God in a bible. letting him guide you in this Getting to know Jesus as he truly is for you,. Some of us judge another when hiding issue we have our own self. Do not ever think you are better than the other person as many were not loved, or had a bad environment to live in. Yet in them a heart of gold and some not so bitter that they had to endure bad life.

Jesus loves them as he loves you he will be there for you. We can not judge or be jealous of another person. let us walk the path of a door and room in their life, they had to live at times Many would never want want to walk though what another might have had to endure, at all so do not judge another person at all. In many cases, pure evil,Satan takes over a family by being weak and allowing Satan to ruin your life. Many are brought up with no knowledge of God at all. The ten laws of His or that they have a friend and savior in Jesus who loves them.

He is first and He loves you the most. He did not harm you, it was the devil who was looking for souls and got them. Yet it's not too late for your life to change and know the Lord and with you, your family. God is gracious and will go after his lost sheep to know him love him and bless him, Pray that you will know him. The Lord will draw all your sins to him with forgiveness for all mankind salvation Others have been brought up in the Lord, they Lack nothing yet, so it seems yet have had evil come upon them in some way yet overcame it with the lord. as all in life time seem to have been and will be attack by a evil of some sort, yet some have a tendency to want to stay clear of a brother or sister that had a horrible life and has nothing. Know that God wants you to reach out and help. Be a blessing in the lives of others whom God wants you to love and help.

As a worker for the Lord for many years, I have had the opportunity to see God, through intercession prayers, change things. He has such great power. I have seen him take another to walk again the power of the lord is strong.Man seems to have forgotten that there is a God. yet we are part if him and he has gifted us all. Just put him first, Man now listens to cults and believes in dark magic. It was a shock to see witchcraft and to know it was truly real. It was through fervent prayers and the Lord's healing that finally took the effects off of the person. The life they had was so badly affected by the darkness. As soon as the person was healed, their family's life became entirely different. When the sickness left, even the things around the yard were restored. Not only did their house become a home again but it brought back a love bond that seemed to have been lost. We are the salt of the earth and I saw how this worked.

The Lord sent us Pray with "salt" for healing. And it has healed crack addiction when placed under the tongue and with prayers to Jesus to take the addiction away after giving yourself to Him and repenting of your sins. You then have to go through this healing with the salt. Others witnessed such works that in India they used to give hyper people salt baths. We are the salt of the earth. Salt has numerous healing properties and so should we as Jesus called us to be the "salt" of the earth. Many can witness for the addiction of drugs crack, other the use of pray with salt. All good comes from God all evil from Satan. yet many a time he will make you think something is good when evil just for you to sin.

God loves and blesses us all. There is God the Father and the Son Jesus and the Holy Spirit making them the Holy Trinity. I can attest to the love and the gifts of the Lord and the spiritual baptism. I bore witness to a lot of miracles. If this was not true, I will tell you so but it is true! God appears to be lost to many and others do not follow Him.

Today, civil unrest seems to be starting across America. The message to me is very clear, the nations of the world will need to be in touch with each other. People from all walks of life, from different faiths, need to realize there is a Holy Spirit and a Lord who loves us all. We need to remember about the prophesied Tribulation or Armageddon, of a war between good and evil. A Rapture with Jesus is going to come. And with the imminent signs of the times...it will come soon. I have been trying to get this message since December 2019, however, the coronavirus happened, then the riots. I hope to get this book out in God's time.

We have lost so many lives in American and around the globe. We are now unified in this fight against the coronavirus. Many of our brothers and sisters of other nations are suffering this as well. Some nations were able to quickly contain the virus and may not have suffered the same losses as we did. They were able to restrain the virus and their citizens have not yielded to riots. They have not gone from town to town, city to city, with destruction and damage.

Lest we forget, these riots are spreading the virus as quickly, going from place to place. We have lost so many lives, not only through the coronavirus but through how we reacted to it. Americans seem to overlook the real crisis here. We have turned away from God and as a godless nation, we seem to forget that God is providence Himself. When we are out of our comfort zones we become violent. We seek to blame our government. We need to understand that the corona-virus is man-made. These riots are led by men. Not God! Our government, no matter who may get in office, will still be facing this dilemma. And if riots do not stop, we will be in for a huge shock. Evil is lurking all over the lands as it sweeps many areas of the nations.

We must comprehend that harming our leaders, our fellow citizens, going out in the streets to kill, to destroy will only cause our deaths and we may go to hell with it. Just because you are a leader of a nation you do not have the right by God to destroy the life He made. In fact there was a Peace agreement signed by other leaders of Nations agreed to not have destructive weapons, which was followed through by former deceased honorable President Bush Sr. God rest his soul, and yet it was broken later. This was and still a true calling from our lord. to save life not take it Therefore not one leader of Nations can by God start or want to and try and to do destroy life he made to have destructive weapons Weapons of mass destruction. all against the true calling of the lord.

The laws of God are Divine and superior. This usually conflicts with the laws of man. There are governments whose laws are so anti-life. Their officials managed to create laws that would destroy or kill a new born child. They would face judgment from the Lord. The spirit of the child is from God regardless of how it got here. We belong to Him first and should in an ideal world, end up with Him. But in the real world, we can also end up with Satan in hell. Abortion is against the lord. if a women life is in danger or the child then a decision need to be made, yet if only want this abortion, not to want the baby, maybe a one night stand and young and not able to take on the responsibly under no cause should you abortion to the child that is God first, give birth to the child if you do not want the baby allow others to have the child some in a family, friends or to the adoption but let it have a life. In a lifetime you may be able to see the child again many finding other now through DNAs,

Save your soul, which is important and give birth to the child if you do abortion is is against the lord save your soul really and give the child a chance to have life and most have wonderful life. if you change your mind the moment you see the child and want the baby keep it there are ways in the system that you be able to keep the child if on drugs. give it up under foster care till you are better of the drug then take your child. you will love. and love you. anyone promoting abortion are against the lord. Yet as I have told all, the lord is the judge of us all. so let it to him.

Gays with healings

Are you gay, none want to face this healings as In pray first found out in pray for a young man who did not want to be gay he wanted to kill himself for being gay in pray I found he had a hormone imbalance guided him to a doctor,he did as the doctor gave him shots he felt normal with out the rage in himself. Others who ask,me to pray for two young women one left her husband leaving even their children family to be gay with another.

In pray for them we found out they had a hormone imbalance went to doctor to confirm and they did given the right treatment are fine now living a normal life. not all have this imbalance. others to find out variety,of reasons some being fear. to have a child. some rejection of the sex they were by a parent. some abused, and some just feeling not loved or understood and fell into another who comfort them and gay themself others were used, taken in to be used.

Some in the world became to be killers in the world who were abused by gay men, turn and killed all gays they knew, as bad as it seems or is to another to the lord who has love and mercy forgive all and heal all if you want to be heal you can be and will. yet have to be honest to this all, Yes, even a killer in our world, abuse happens to many who do not get the proper help, who do not have love, or someone to turn to. as mamy not know Jesus and all he himself had to suffer. are left in rages. and to harm another.

They need help, and Jesus of him in the right understanding of life. his love and his forgiveness. as many are subject to abuse and unfortunately are in mental hospital or conditions all of their live. and others with right treatment and a godly person to talk with them they will be well again, with this and right medicine to some to help them live a normal life again.

Doing a selected radio show to help anyone who was gay who did not want to be gay. they said, they did not care, they wanted to be gay. so the choice is theirs. We love all in life, and it is up to them and choice they have and judge by God. I just passed information I did find. out just as in life others sin over desperation they not do if not desperate. once they tell the lord who is a understanding God repent set free Yet we all get judge by our lord. yet many did not want to be gay, and with knowledge God send for others to have and my self found out in pray there were hormone imbalance to many that felt they were born gay and not. As much in life now can go into the womb of a mother before birth to find some defects if not a child from ten on should be check for this as well as knowledge of abuse in the world and open to others to vent this to open up to another or a group of others in order to now harbor abuse that happened to them which will only bring on in many cases a mental condition.

In my opinion, with the recent discoveries and breakthroughs, we can determine if a pregnancy will endanger life or lives. If bearing this child would affect either the mother or the child or both...there should be a choice to either go through with it or not. However, for most the reason to abort, technically kill, a child is for selfish reasons, this is offensive. If one just wants to remain fabulous and in great shape, this is not a reason at all.

For cold and heartless reasons, if a mother or the father has no love in them at all (many seem in the world to have gotten this way) yet the lord is the judge they face God's judgment. Some if they find out it is a girl or a boy they did not want, they go for an abortion. This child is God's and it is truly a sin to do this. many say its my life, my body and my choice. yes, and the lord is the judge of it all. All we can do is try to help, be there give reasons not to do abortion of a child. as some later reject it some hold such guilt and can not seem to have good life for self, and some can not have a child again. sad, most I have met regretted it.

I remember a time during the delivery of my daughter. The nurse told me to pull the baby back in. Please know, if anyone asks you to do this, hold your baby back, do not do this. This can cause brain damage. I learned this from my grandmother and others in the medical field. Do not hold your baby back, just keep on giving your child birth I am happy today that I did listen. When the nurse told me to do this, I did not listen. Today, my beautiful daughter is well. My delivery of her was quick. I wonder if I did what the nurse asked me to do, I may most likely have had a child with damage to her brain. This baby was presumed to be a tube baby during my initial prenatal check-ups. But with prayers, she actually rolled

The Great I AM I AM

into the right place for her to develop and be born. Prayer works and I am grateful for the knowledge shared by many in my life. For the love and goodness of their hearts, I was prepared. If it were someone who may have been naive and did what the nurse asked, the outcome may have been different. I don't blame the nurse, it is not her fault, she may not have known in those days the technology wasn't as advanced as it is today. I and my daughter were blessed to have someone tell me. I pass this knowledge along to as many others so you would know.

A child is a blessing! You may not want the child you have in your belly right now but when you hold this child in your arms, you will know it was all worth it. I was blessed to have three children.

We may take life for granted and forget that life is precious. Life is from God. He has shaped us and created us in His image and likeness. I desired to serve God. this was my heart desire as a child And by His grace, I can do so in this lifetime. Our beautiful lord did bless me with 3 children. I love them and am so happy and proud of them all. I have had 3 a near-death experience and to be alive and see them after so many years of longing, is a blessing.

I am grateful for God gave me back my life. He saw to it that a wonderful black family would take care of me. I love the Lord. He leads me to live and not to die homeless in a street. I honor Him, I praise Him, and thank the Lord for all He did for me. I did have to go through so much, yes. Yet I did go through every hurdle, failure, and mistake, hurt abuse rejections bad health 3 near death, homeless loss of my children I was raising alone hospitals. sadness, etc. yet the lord pulled me through later I my taught my children of Jesus did much with them worship together I did not have a TV we did arts crafts nature walks and all activity skying they did sports and talents nights watching the stars and talking of their dreams to be in life..my loves I wanted to be with and work hard for I did my best to teach them a positive life they were brought up without a father who wanted a different life to live, yet they had Jesus as there heavenly father then my health failed again i did get heal of all issue much truma much fear, much loss much sins of mistakes I did make along with much more. and to face jealous of other in my life to me I often wondered if they had to walk the walk I had to walk I truly do not believe they want to open the door to it. Jesus brought me through and saw other for my life. to do with him and for him to show me teach me he was first in my life nothing no one but Jesus is first in my life.

As he gifted me as a child and much more later to serve him the desire of my heart as a child growing up I had to learn that Jesus was first he baptized me in his holy spirit it was beautiful as i felt his spirit inward to fill me with his energy and his wonderful love. He gifted me more in the spiritual gifts. as later he guided me to serve him for over 27 years each day to use my gifts to help others in my life. and still do,

Through this book, I am reaching out to all across the Nations who our lord loves and wants with him, every one of you. His precious spirit came upon me to write on The Great Tribulation the Rapture. I did so with love and with sorrow. Life is precious, we should not take it for granted. I see so many lives taken by this terrible virus, the lives destroyed and taken by the riots. and all life lost in other Nations as well. along with riots to take life from another even children my heart goes out to, I see those who are dying daily in the streets.

Remember, you can only truly help another out of love in your heart. Unleash the love you do have in your heart and reach to another so we can break this evil force set forth by Satan. myself I do go out at times not as i did years ago but I still do. for anyone who is hungry, and pray for another we are needed and you can reach out as well. In the days of now I have another stand back from me as i do a pray for them and use my gifts for this. i hand food in a paper bag to others. or bring blanket for them or umbrellas, We are all needed and lord says if you do for my least of your brothers you are doing for me, some time you will meet a angle. they appear and in one glance gone vanish it is so odd. but happens to many of us in all sorts of ways.

The Great I AM I AM

When you are in a dilemma of whether to keep your child. Seek God. This child may turn out to be the greatest delight you would ever have in your life. Girls are wonderful and so are boys. And God has His reasons for the choice of whom he was going to give you in your life. His reasons are always superior to ours. We do not have the right to do abortions when others out there seek to adopt children because they were not lucky to have one of theirs. They can provide and give your child a good life. If ever it comes to that, there are systems in place, and adoptive parents do go through a series of tests and interviews. Your child will be given them to adjust as they will be given time with the child before they adopt. Now they have open adoptions where the mother can visit the child every so many months.

To have a child is a blessing and there are ways to help with childbirth pain and many as I did myself have had a natural childbirth. There were classes on how to have them and professionals who see you through it all. Pain during childbirth, yes. But the joy of holding him or her in your arms will be all worth it. If you have had an unwanted pregnancy, then remember others have prayed and longed for one. Life is sacred. Maybe through you, a couple will be blessed with your child. If you do not like your life change, you have options.

You can seek help from many organizations out there and a God that made you. Seek His help, God is good, always. Recognize that we have a wonderful Jesus who loves us and who will forgive everything. If you had no concept of this, maybe a bit naive, or is an innocent victim, then it's not your fault. Jesus will forgive us of all things the moment we ask Him to do so and He will bless us as well. He is the judge and He is the One we will face in the final door; He forgives all sins we do and He is the judge of them all.

All human life is precious. You may be the leader of a nation and whatever your opinion is, it is not going to change this. Every war waged, every bomb explosion and every life extinguished too soon because of you, is not of God. Hold your peace and work it. Join the

United Nations for peace and harmony. God once said No More war in my world. a call from the lord.

I am not the greatest writer, and I am not a world-renowned scholar. I am just a simple being inspired to write. The Lord gets all the Glory before His messages and healing and love for us all. We must unite in brotherhood all over the world in spirit of His love as His love made us all. We must overcome Evil by Satan. Know that he is in this world. By joining together in peace, love, trusting in Jesus first as He will with us. And yes, the lord did gift me as a child as he gifts us all. in spiritual yes my hearts desire was to serve him one day and I did have and am. I am just living life and loving people. Yes, Satan tried to destroy me, more than once. And Yes, God stepped in, and here I am. Blessed with life with so many experiences and stories to tell to witness of him, I was led by God to write this book and my only desire is to be able to share the Great I AM I AM. I want to share it with as many others, in this nation and other nations. I pray to send forth a message. With love and hope, to help and touch as many lives and to prepare us for the Tribulation (Armageddon) Rapture.

With a special prayer that one day we all be in the wonderful new world of the healing of the lands most of all yet to be in a Rapture of Jesus! As we all held on to him with the bond of love, may we repent to Him and sin no more. He has forgiven us of all, may we all enter into the Rapture. For years there has been hate, discrimination, along with jealousy, control, power plays. We may have been with many relations in life who have been following evil Satan, with no love of God. We are not superior to anyone. We are subject to our Maker and His laws. He wants us all to honor Him and to love one another as He making us all. With His love in all men's hearts.

"United we stand and divided we fall. we are all God's creations" YGOL.

We are all in this together as Nations of God's people and we must pray to stay strong, because of the many evil that has been laid upon us. We must reach out to all nations to extend peace with one another. Let us pray for the entire earth's well-being. God is not a God of evil. He does not want us to make evil weapons to kill the life He made.

Satan wants us to hate, to think we have power over a loving God that gave us life. Satan wants us to fight to kill. He has ordered for us to not have water or food or land. He has set evil forces to keep us apart from one another. To hurt, to hate, to want to destroy. When we can truly network all our needs through organizations like the United Nations and channel and help one another to have a better life throughout the earth.

There are ways for healing the land. Through God and by His plans we find irrigation. To fill the earth with food and drinks. He has made every one of us uniquely and we should share our talents to make a better world. We are to find ways to help the economy, to grow and prosper together, all nations together. Uniting in progress for one another. God is a generous God who wants us to share the land and waterways. and to pipe the water to the area that need the irrigation for all to eat, drink, have and live and be happy this as well as was a calling from our lord given in 1990's YGOL we still need to do this.

We need to join hands for our world and to get crime off our communities and streets. Together we can put our nations under control. Let us get rid of drugs! Let it be gone and a thing in the past. May we focus and concentrate on ways to keep each other healthy and to prosper in positive ways. May our lives be for Him. To honor God, who made us. He loves you. He offered His Only Son, Jesus who suffered for all of us. Everyone sins and so let no stone be tossed. We are all sinners and we must do our best not to sin again and repent to God. The Father said to repent to Jesus to be forgiven. To forgive and follow a good way of life for us to go to heaven after our physical death here. Let us do our best not to listen to the lies of this devil. He takes pleasure in putting our lives in chaos and taking our souls. He pushes us to do drugs and evil ways. He takes delight in making us miserable.

Love will break an evil force, so reach out and love the Lord, our families, and others in the world. Talk about love, spread it through words and actions. If Satan tries to pull you down through others who may harm you, abuse you, reject you. Do not allow it to drag you down. Let us not be stuck in this merry-go-round of hell. The devil will entice you and lie to you to do drugs to take your pain away. It does not work! Drugs will not numb you from the pain, it will entrench you deeply so he could gain your soul. Face your problems. It could be rejection or a mistake you did. Be forgiving to yourself. Seek Jesus and He will help you as He did me and others. Christ died on the cross, crucified. We should thank the Lord for in His Death He has set us free.

The drug you are taking will not erase your difficulties. Be strong! You have it in you to do this. You are worth dying for. The Lord Jesus did that for us. Always remember, Jesus is first and He loves you more than anyone can ever love you. Jesus is first and I want you to know this, it took me to lose all that I had, be homeless on a street with a month to live. All rejected me. No one tried to reach out to me. Jesus is the only one who would not reject me. When I called out to Him, He shaped my life so that I didn't fall into the evilness of Satan. He took my hand to be triumphant over drugs and not end up in prostitution or other crimes.

Cling unto the Lord and allow Him to take you, help you, and heal you. He will find ways to do so. He is God and He will not abandon you. Go to Him and tell Him you need Him. Love Him and ask Him for His forgiveness. Ask Him to heal you by giving your entire life to Him. Let His will be your will. "My will, Lord, will be Your will. Keep me strong and protect me against evil as I reject it out of my life." Be honest and you will be strong and whatever Satan did to get you and will continue to do so until he breaks you and take you to hell. And he will.

We are the salt of the earth. I was healed by the Lord, He used and guided me to be a salt. Salt and its healing powers. I saw witchcraft leave a person by pray use of salt in alll healigs pray to the lord as he guide the pray yet all healing from Jesus is done with pray to him first. he hiself used even mud in a healing he was doing from his father who gifted him as he is Jesus and had a purpose as we all have a purpose and he like us all are one of a kind. pray was used to keep off from drugs. I saw the Lord do extraordinary healing and so with so many other witnesses for many years and it is real. The Lord loves us all that he supplied us with healing minerals readily available in nature. now as well. Yet do with pray as well. and to doctors the Lord has given the love the knowledge the gifts to help another yet still pray,.

We are to love Him and one another. Do you fear another race? For their color? Or the way they look? Remember, we are all created by the One True God and in truth, we are all the same. Our awareness of others or how we see another race is a test from the Lord. From time to time, He wants to see your reaction to another race. Does it matter what color of one's skin is? Or that a person's hair is different from yours? We all are different, even if we have the same skin color or race.

Do we think we are better than the other races? The fact is many of our brothers and sisters from other races and creeds are intelligent, talented, and creative humans. Knowledge, wisdom, experience, and cultural differences should bring diversity. It is how the world is so that we can gain from one another. Our desire should be geared towards helping one another and loving each other's differences. It should bring out the love in one's heart and we should as the Lord said, greet one another with a "holy kiss." We are all His.

Let not the color, race, and differences deter us from and going back to Him. Let us return to God and hope for Him to say, "Job well done! Come and enter into my kingdom.

Whatever the skin color of your neighbor is, let love shine in your heart. We have problems that we all face. Everyone has a different upbringing, or, culture and ways. There are some with bigger problems and it would be much better not to judge them by their color. Instead, spread the love by offering your hand. Be a beacon and let them witness Jesus through you. Even if you feel they are unworthy. Even if you see that they are full of hate.

Do something nice today for someone. Bake a cake or cookies for that little girl who lives next door. Or sew something up for that neighbor who never smiles back at you. Pray and ask the Lord, He will tell you what to do. Visit your other neighbor, perhaps they need you. In your prayer say, "Show me, Lord, what you would have for me to do today. Wait and listen. Do it and be encouraged to do the same on a daily.

Let this not stop you from going further. Your heart will desire more. Feed the homeless. Reach out to those who have ended up in the streets. You never know what life threw at them. Be generous as God has been to you.

Satan has been tempting us and lying to us for generations. He has done so from generation to generation starting from Adam and Eve. When Eve disobeyed the Lord it was because Satan tempted Eve. And Eve got to Adam, they were cast out of "The Garden of Eden". And the sin that was started then, we have it in all of us. Generation to generation curse. We need to pray for it to end.

Generational curses

Have you read about generational curses? It is written in Exodus 34:7 "the iniquity of the fathers on the children and the children's children, to the third and fourth generation." GENERATIONAL CURSES is handed down from one generation to the next. They call it a curse, because it a chain reaction of either abuse, or, health issues, or, mental or physical or hate, or even discrimination. It is a case of upbringing and seeing what the parents or grandparents are doing. It can be the emotional effect of parents' divorces. The mental, physical, sexual, or emotional abuses from parents might be instilled in the subconscious of certain families. This can also be said of alcoholism and drugs. So the question is, are we made responsible for the sins of our fathers? Of course not! If you turn to Jesus, you will see a huge difference in your life.

However, we need to note that the original sin that ousted us from paradise had us cursed. Remember how Adam and Eve have been expelled from The Garden of Eden? That made all of us slaves to sin. And praises to God, He offered His Only Son so that we could be redeemed from the sinfulness of our first parents. With this said, our salvation will be the choice we make of whether or not we entrust ourselves to Jesus.

Jesus loves us all, we are His and He wants us to be with Him. He can touch our lives, change us and give us our heart's desires. Follow Him. Love and prayers can break the generational curse.

Pray for the Armor of God

We must put on the armor of God daily on us. Put on the Shoes of Peace wherever you go, the Belt of Truth to keep us honest in life, the Breastplate of Righteousness to do what is right and to remain right by God, the Helmet of Salvation that we may always think of the salvation of our souls, and out from your mouth, the Sword of the Tongue. Our sword so that we say things of love and honesty. And finally, bring the Hedge of Protection with us daily.

Consciously go over these in your mind and you can even do it with your children. Prepare your day with these armors. Pray, honor the Lord, repent for your salvation daily. The Great I AM I AM has not gone out yet, over a year in trying to get this out to all. We are know with another President Biden as we pray for blessing for him God wanted him in office as he did President Trump in office for the lord's reasons not ours we must all concede to this and accept it.

Our Lord has a reason for former Presidents he has in office that truly only the lord knows of the reason, Let us go on, Yet let us know that former President Trump did a great work, and was not at all responsible for a deadly virus we have today a man -made one and our President did not do. he was and is not a doctor and at the time of the onset even doctor did not know the full effects of this. and once our President did know he did react quick in life other Presidents were warned of evil in the police force and in other organization that did not react fast or not at all. not to think or truly realize this to be so. yet was and harmed many,

Evil will seep into all if it can, but many have turn to evil for greed for power for hate much negative reason let other know this is wrong and others to refrain from evil as it is from Satan and if warned of it to come then respond to this with Gods love and his knowledge.

He is coming in a bad time in the world. as we can only pray for the healing of the lands and love one to one another all over the Nations for we do not know the hour, the day, the time we have for a Great Tribulation and Rapture, this book was guided to write and on the realm of this to happen with love and pray is sent out to others. to help one to be prepared of this time and healing for others who are very block from themselfs who are in addiction or abuse can be one as well in a generation curse some healings to help another on our way,

The Great I AM I AM is not to judge anyone as the only one at the end of our last door of life to open iis a wonderful God that loves us, He will be the judge of us all. Yet we must know all of us there is a evil devil and many may not make it to the lord but to be with Satan as the lord wants us to know right from wrong a sin and evil and a satan that wants your soul belong to Jesus who will bring you to the Rapture as you do not allow Satan to fool and harm your soul to hell. Praying all God hear s all pray and will guide you and answer all pray be faithful to him have faith as all pray are answered in his time not ours and in the meantime follow him.

There was foresight years ago of the evil force that got into the police force department with this warning of this. not to increase asking to check forces for stress, power plays, mental illness, drugs, and decimations, etc.

This was given to the President office Vice President office; they may have just ignored. as nothing was being done. As evil kept continuing to take over, Check the statistic of this to be true, be assured, this evil was and is not just pined pointed on just for blacks, race.

This force of evil,"Satan," has increased since then, as the devil is trying to take over others all others in all Nations under God with all people, he made. Satan wants us to do evil and take souls to him THIS MUST STOP, it is not of God who loves and wants us to love one-another, having a prosperous life, know where it is coming from before it takes over you. we all must stay strong against all sorts of evil by not giving into to evil.

Evil is not of God and all Nations people must realize and know this. Satan hates love, and loves evil, discord, loves it for us to hate and go against one another creates wars creates children being killed, harm destroy loves anger and has made man make virus, man-made riots, man-made wars. God wants Peace and love other to help one another evil exist in the world and as many know, will attack us all love has more power than Satan evil as he hates love and for others in all Nations to get along.

We must strive for Peace from God as we rebuke, putting Satan with no Power at all. Get to your inner strength and do all to rebuke him, to strive for peace, for love of God his ways of love Peace with care to help one another to stop this evil force coming among all, can this be done

Yes, it can be done. Stopped. by us and all Leaders of all Nations to not kill power play, destroy greed, decimation we are all loved and made by God. No one has a right to take another life or self but the lord who gave us life to start with,

Your Gift of life. was giving by him and work across the Nation for Peace in all Nations of the world. WE all Must change from our evil ways to the ways the walk the light and love in all of us by God. Yes, he had a son of his Jesus and he suffer for all mam sins and to bring them back to the father path of life and heaven our souls we all have to be saved Let us reach out and realize this as we extend ourself to love one another, not torment, hurt, kill and destroy each other Wars, greed, power play, God is over all of us, and he is high looking at all of us. Let us be a Glory to him not a person that against the lord and all for the evil heart harden and cruel devil to only take you to hell.

Remember God made and loves us all and Jesus lived died in such a terrible way man's evil not God who had to show us the evil of Satan who took over the good of a man that evil is in the world we live in we are not in heaven be aware of this and for evil many suffer as Jesus did Yes we must forgive and be forgiven as we go forth for the true will God has for our life and that is not destroying life ours and another. at all.

Let there be no Wars and to network our needs of all Nation in the world we must join in a Peace, not be ignorant and think we are smart and not by doing lies and hurt destroying. we must get evil hate. drugs and addictions out of our life force and greed we must work together on the money value across the globe. once Unity was signed for no more wars in God world in 1991 Peace a true call of the lord. then broken, so we face evil we must uphold the Peace in all our Nations in the world

There are ways to get along. and to do it right. If a Leader of a Nation is evil and not truly help this people and peace with others he must change or leave his office as he is not a honor to God or others in his Nation, and another should be appointed a new leader.

As we face Mexico and other Nation this very moment. This must change and be brought to the UN for counsel as all must step in on this to get rid of drugs to get other to be able to live in the county they are in, to fill the needs to all have counsel of all Nation to do this with honor to God as God made all the land not man. and God gave life not man the air we breathe God and the ground we walk on his given all of us life with his love in us all. SO Let US Join into Gods Peace love not Satan evil to hell.

ALL STOP the evil and rally with love with appreciation of life to the lord to change from evil to good. No more wars in the world God made, networking all needs in all Nation with one another in counsel to agree put knowledge of other to help know how and to join in one accord to do this for the betterment of all mankind. This can be done!

The Ten Commandments of God

EXODUS 20:2-17 (King James Version)

1. I am the Lord thy God, which have brought thee out of the land of Egypt, out of the house of bondage.

2. Thou shalt have no other Gods before me.

3. Thou shalt not make unto thee any graven image, or any likeness of any thing that is in heaven above, or that is in the Earth beneath, or that which is in the water under the Earth. Thou shalt not bow thyself to them, nor serve them: for I the Lord thy God am a jealous God, visiting the iniquity of the fathers upon the children unto the third and fourth generation of them that hate me; And showing mercy unto thousands of them that love me, and keep my commandments.

4. Thou shalt not take the name of the Lord thy God in vain; for the Lord will not hold him guiltless that taketh his name in vain.

5. Remember the Sabbath day, to keep it Holy. Six days shalt thou labor, and do all thy work: But the seventh day is the Sabbath of the Lord thy God: in it thou shalt not do any work, thou, nor thy son, nor thy daughter, thy manservant, nor thy maidservant, nor thy cattle, nor thy stranger that is within thy gates: For in six days the Lord made heaven and earth, and sea and all that in them is, and rested the seventh day: wherefore the Lord blessed the Sabbath day, and hallowed it.

6. Honor thy father and thy mother: that thy days may be long upon the land which the Lord thy God giveth thee.

7. Thou shalt not kill.

8. Thou shalt not commit adultery.

9. Thou shalt not steal.

10. Thou shalt not bear false witness against thy neighbor. Thou shalt not covet thy neighbor's house,   thou shalt not covet thy neighbor's wife, nor his manservant, nor his maidservant, nor his ox, nor his ass, nor anything that is thy neighbor's.

The first two commandments help us to love and honor God. The Law of Love tells us "Love the Lord your God with all your heart, with all your strength, and with all your mind." The last seven commandments help us to love others and ourselves. The Law of Love tells us "Love your neighbor as you love yourself."

Prayers & Thoughts

Now as I close this book, to the darkness, of the night, which has come, we hear the crickets' sounds, the ocean waves splashing against the shore. A moon so full and bright with stars. In distance, we can hear a cat's meow and a dog's bark, a baby's cry. As the night falls with a gentle breeze sweeping on our faces. I smell the aroma of an apple pie, as it circulates through the night sky.

As we finish our day, folded all in the arms of the Lord, you may be with your husband or wife, a family member, or a little pet friend. Thank God for all we have. If you are homeless and only have a rug, or a part of the land to sleep on, look up and watch the moon as it shines above us. Close your eyes and be put to sleep by a Lord who made these wondrous creations.

Let us pray for peace, harmony, and love, to cover the land with the Spirit of the Lord. His spirit to fall upon you. Pray for yourself during this night, that you may sleep in peace, and pray for this night as if it were your last if you should wake up or not. Let His spirit of love touch us each night as we sleep. Let His Spirit of healing come over us. As it rejuvenates our bodies to go on and start a new day in our life. Let us have an endless appreciation of how we live and what we have...may we have endless love for all. of us in all Nations under God.

The End

I want to say thank you to Parchment Global Publishing Family. Josh, Rose, Megan, Mia and all others, thank you for making this possible and my family, sister Regina and Mother Gaston.

- *Maryann*

CPSIA information can be obtained
at www.ICGtesting.com
Printed in the USA
BVHW081105271221
624882BV00006B/170